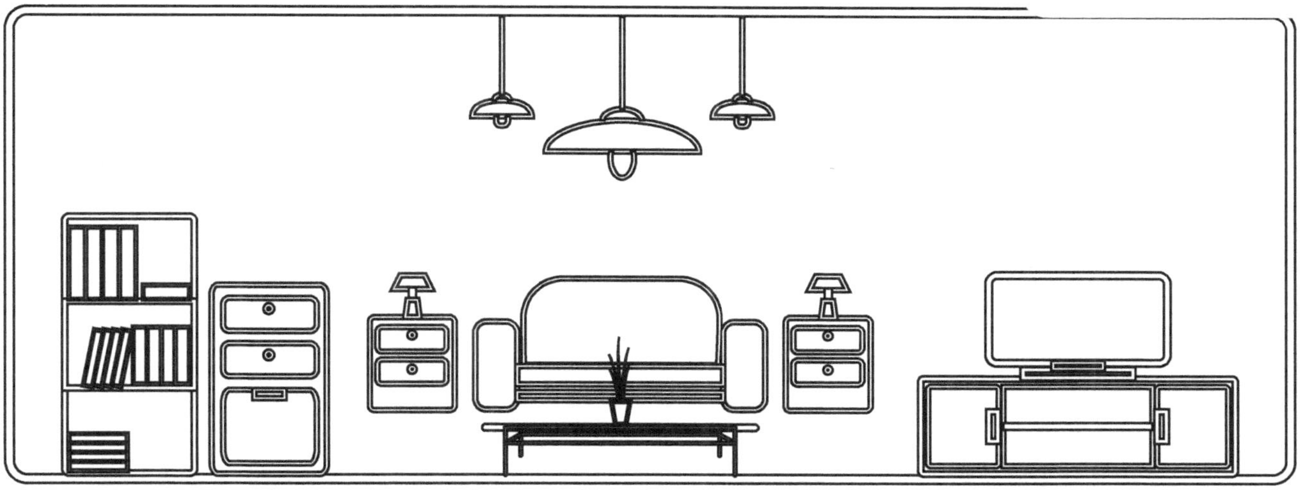

THIS BOOK BELONGS TO :

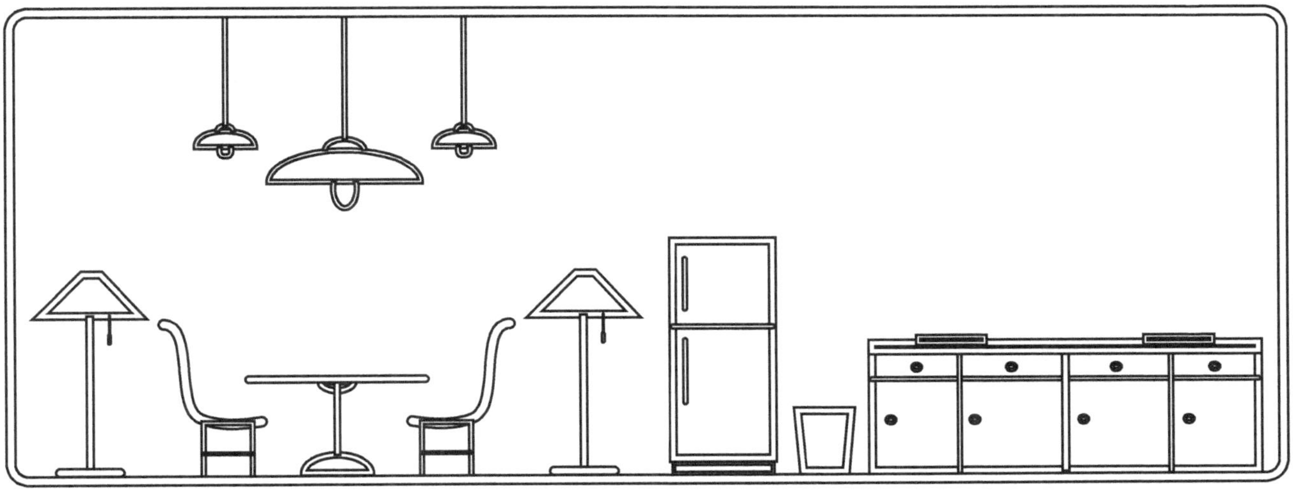

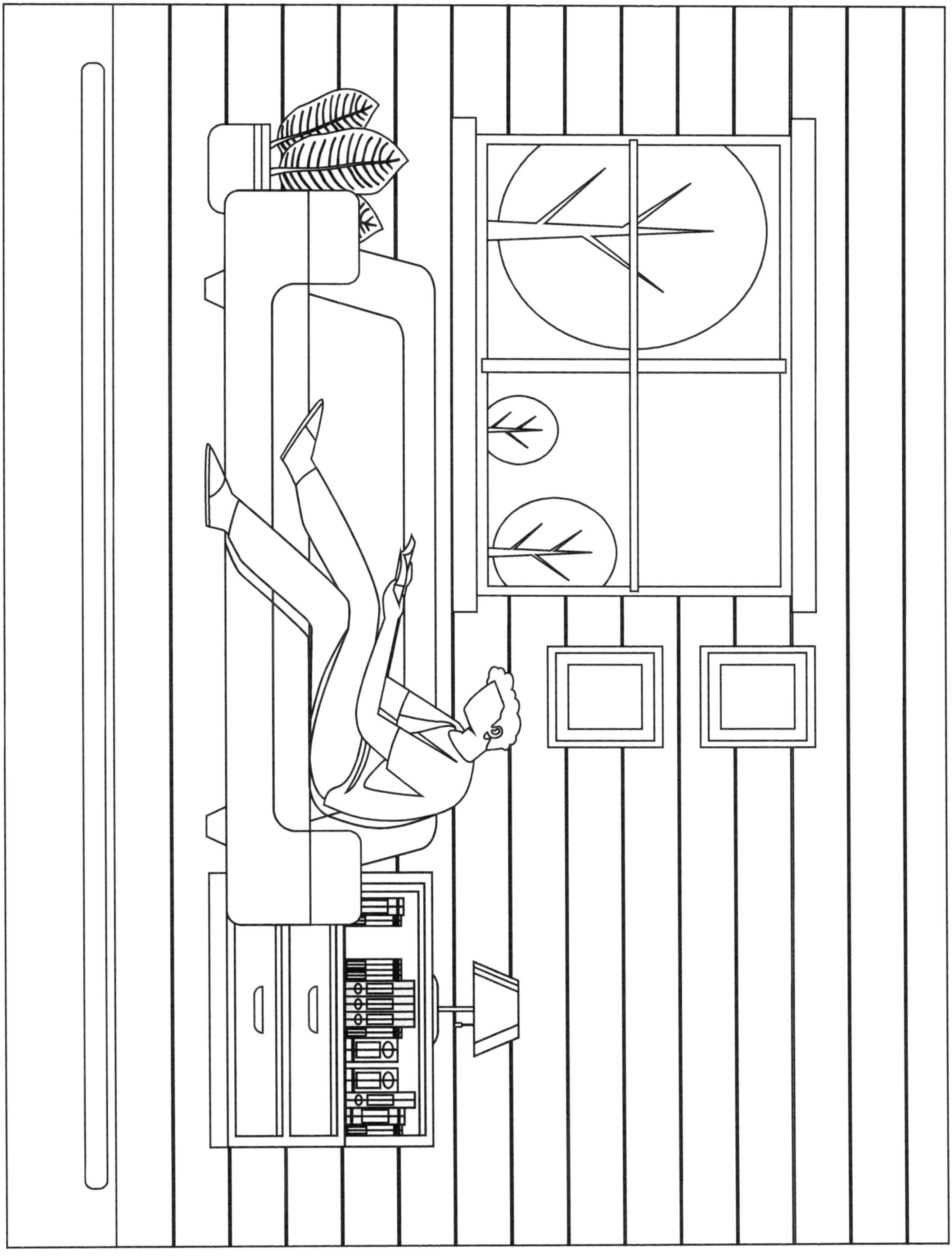

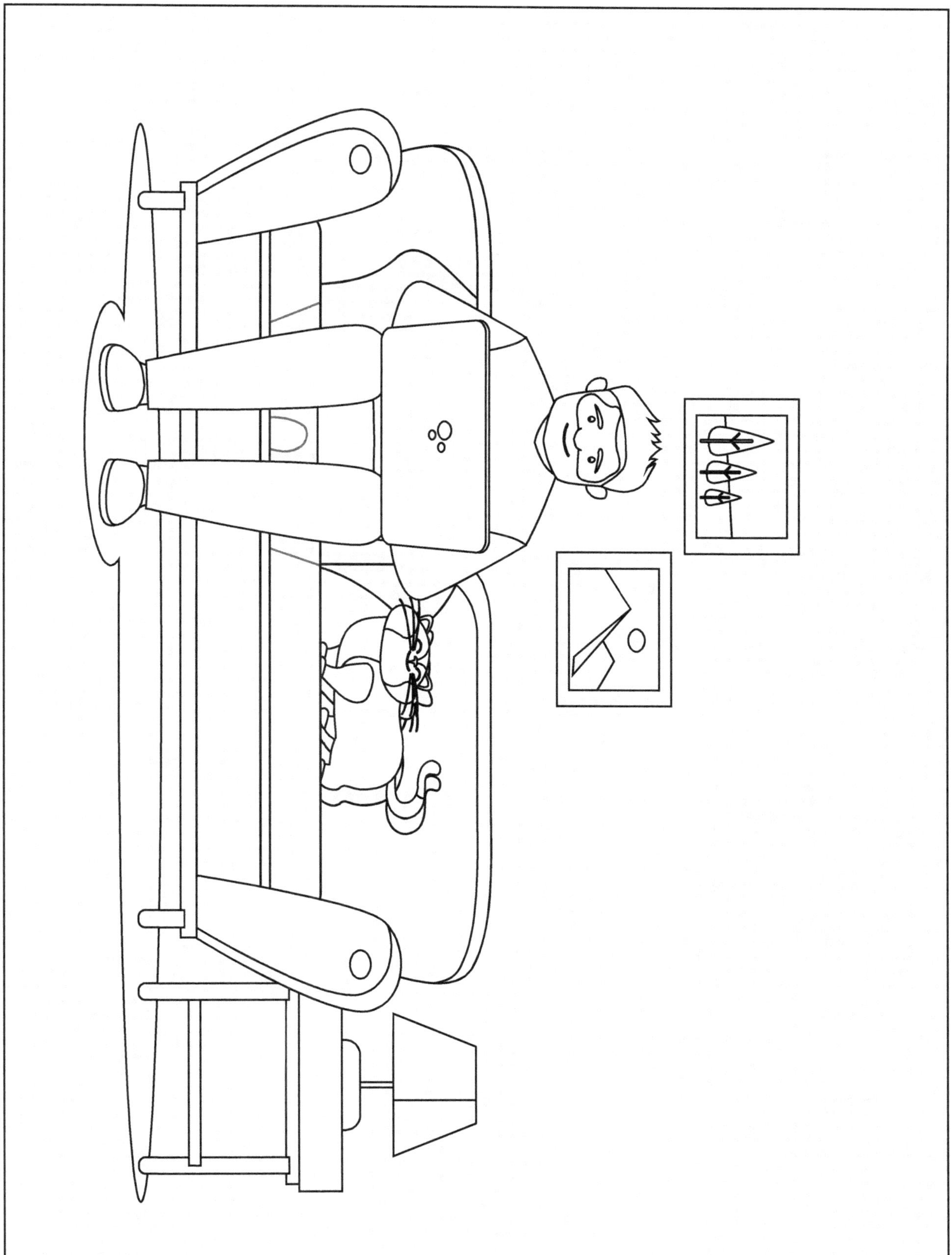

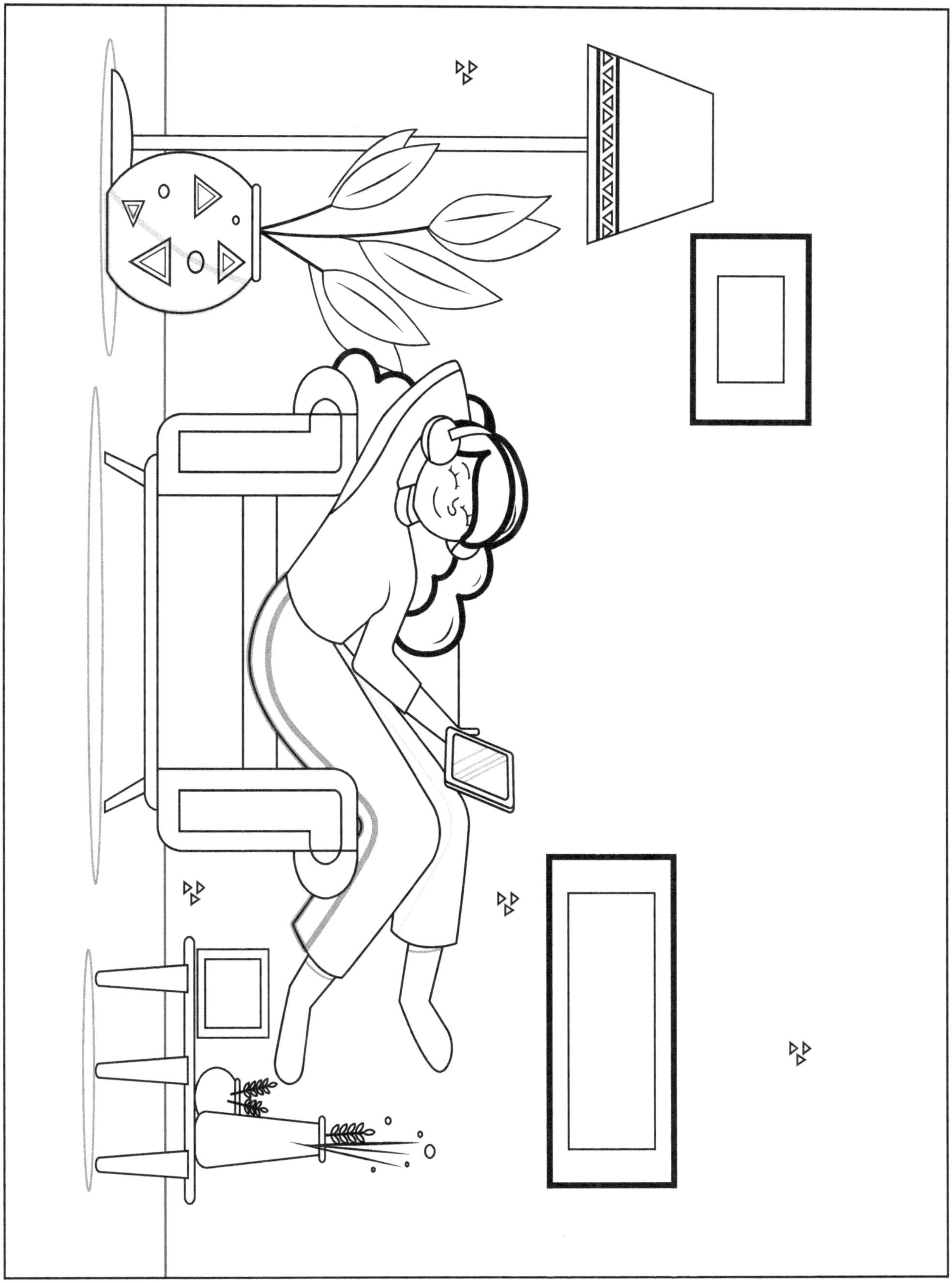

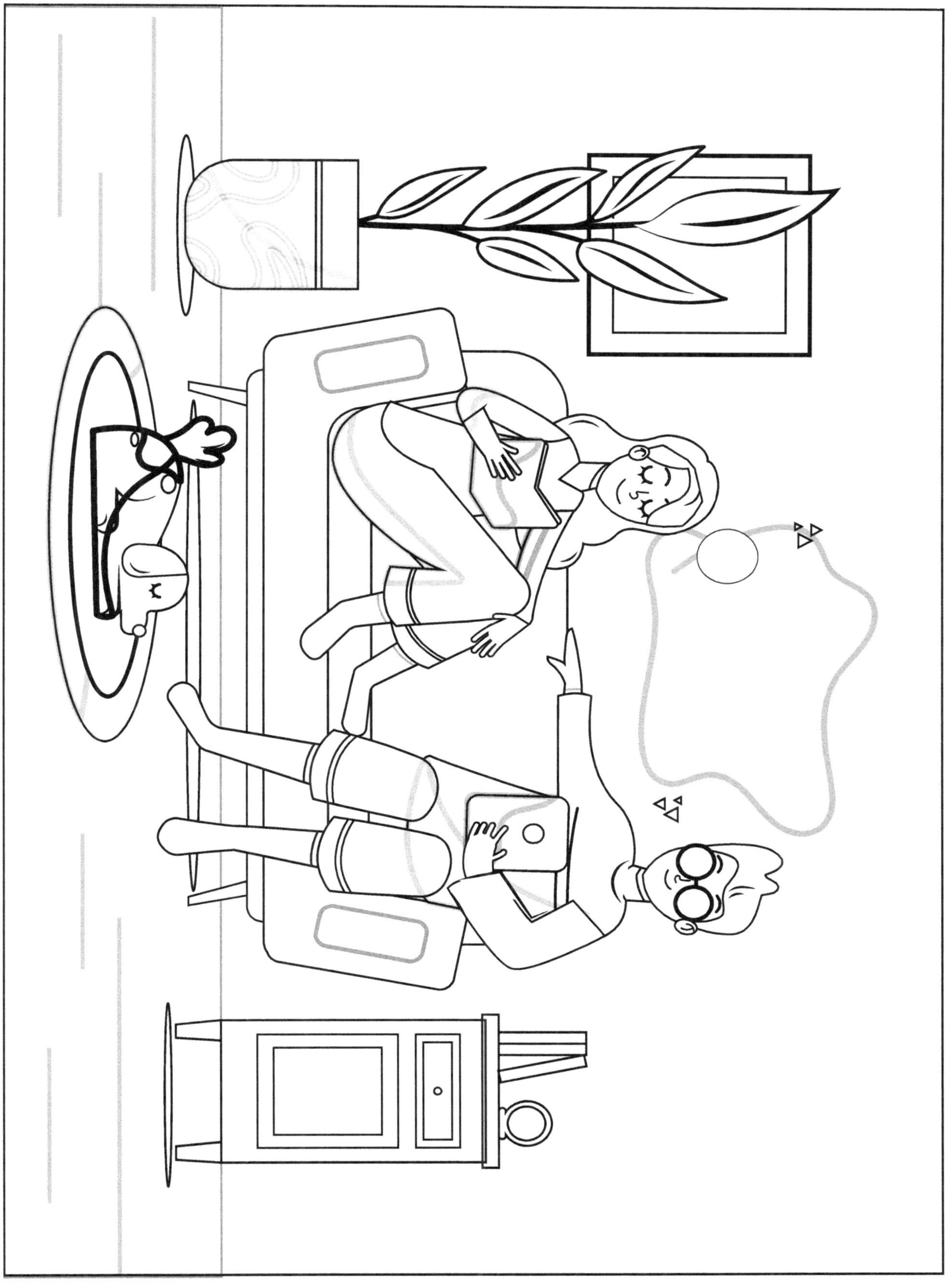

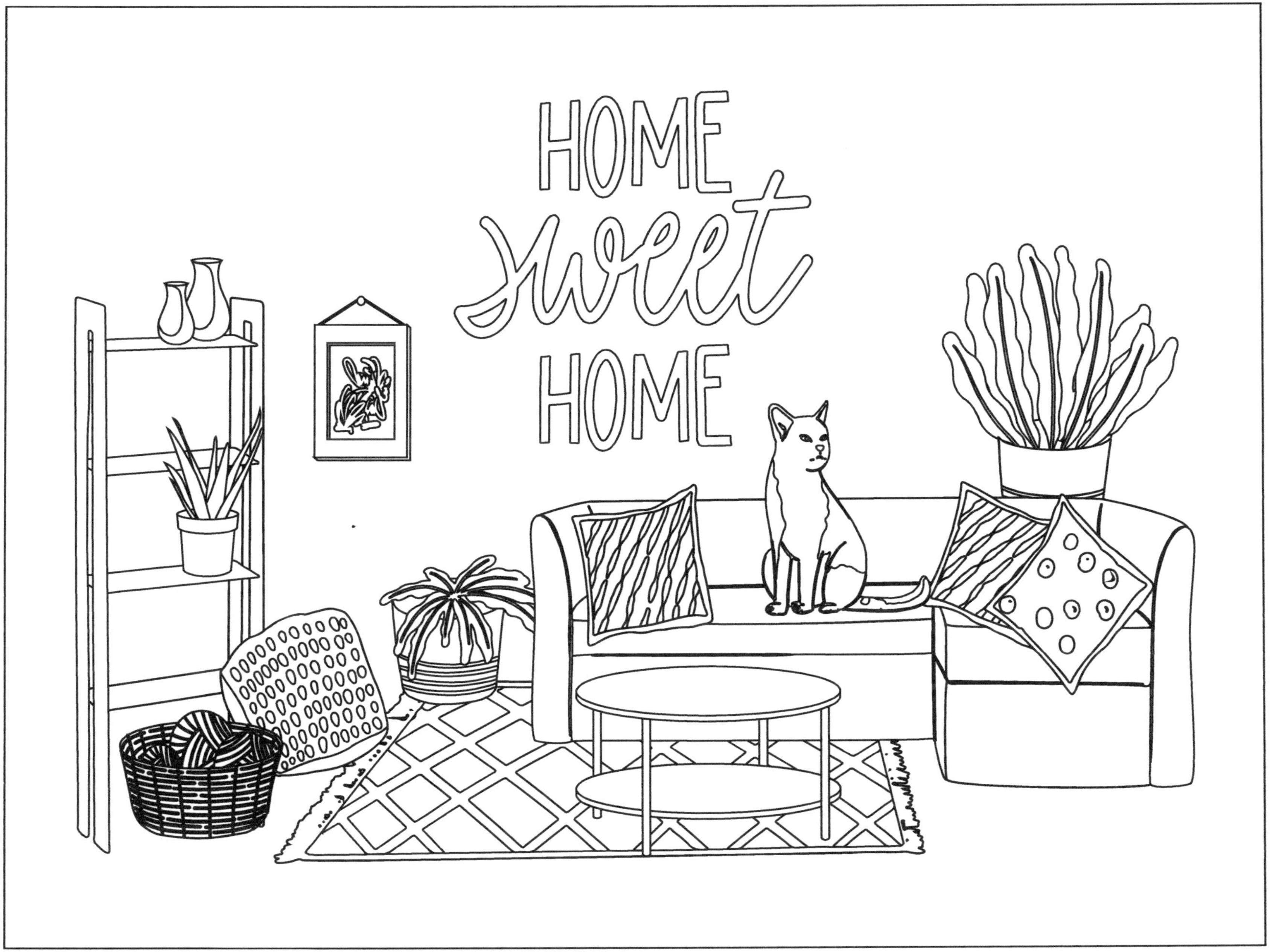
HOME
sweet
HOME

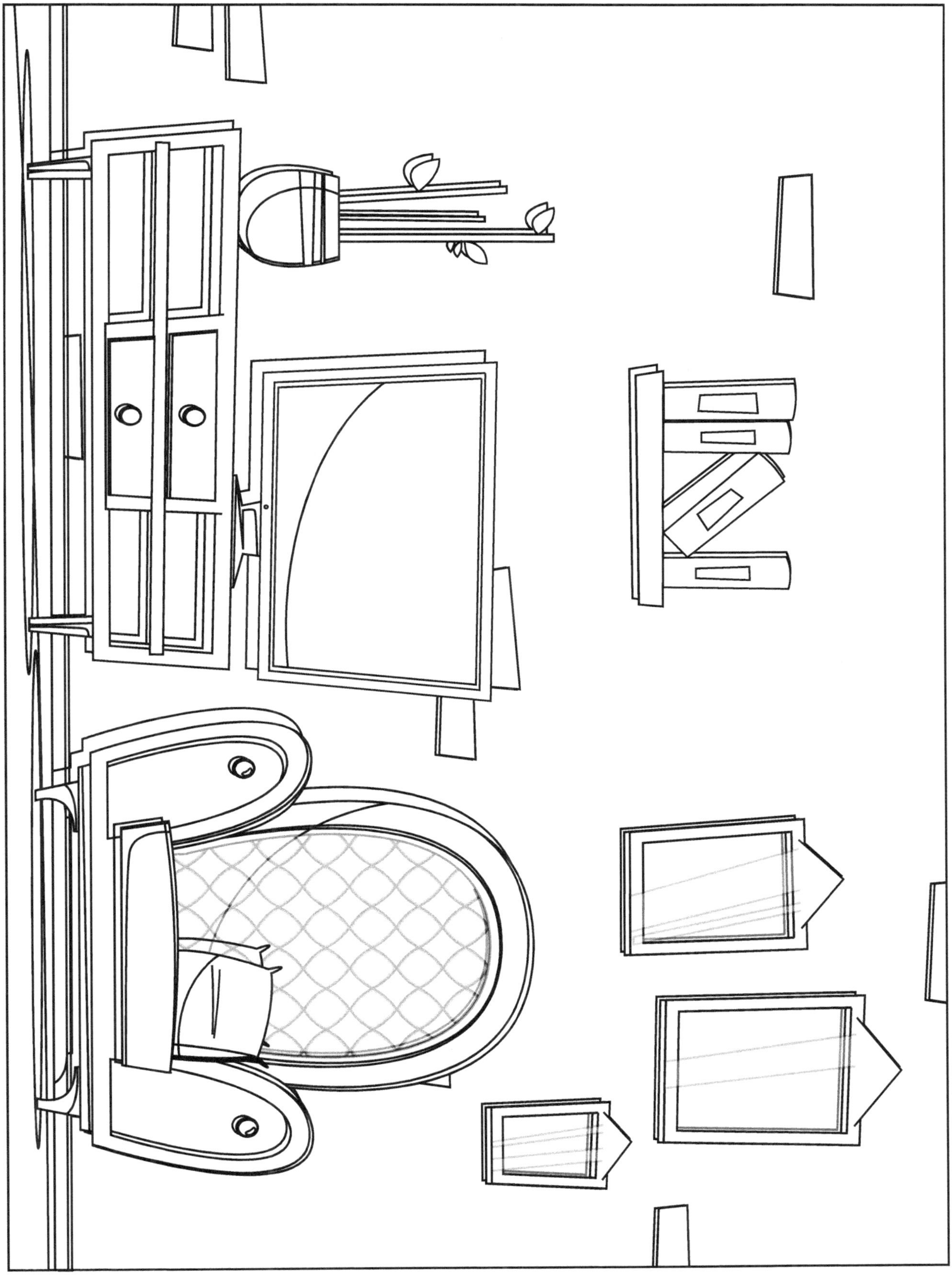

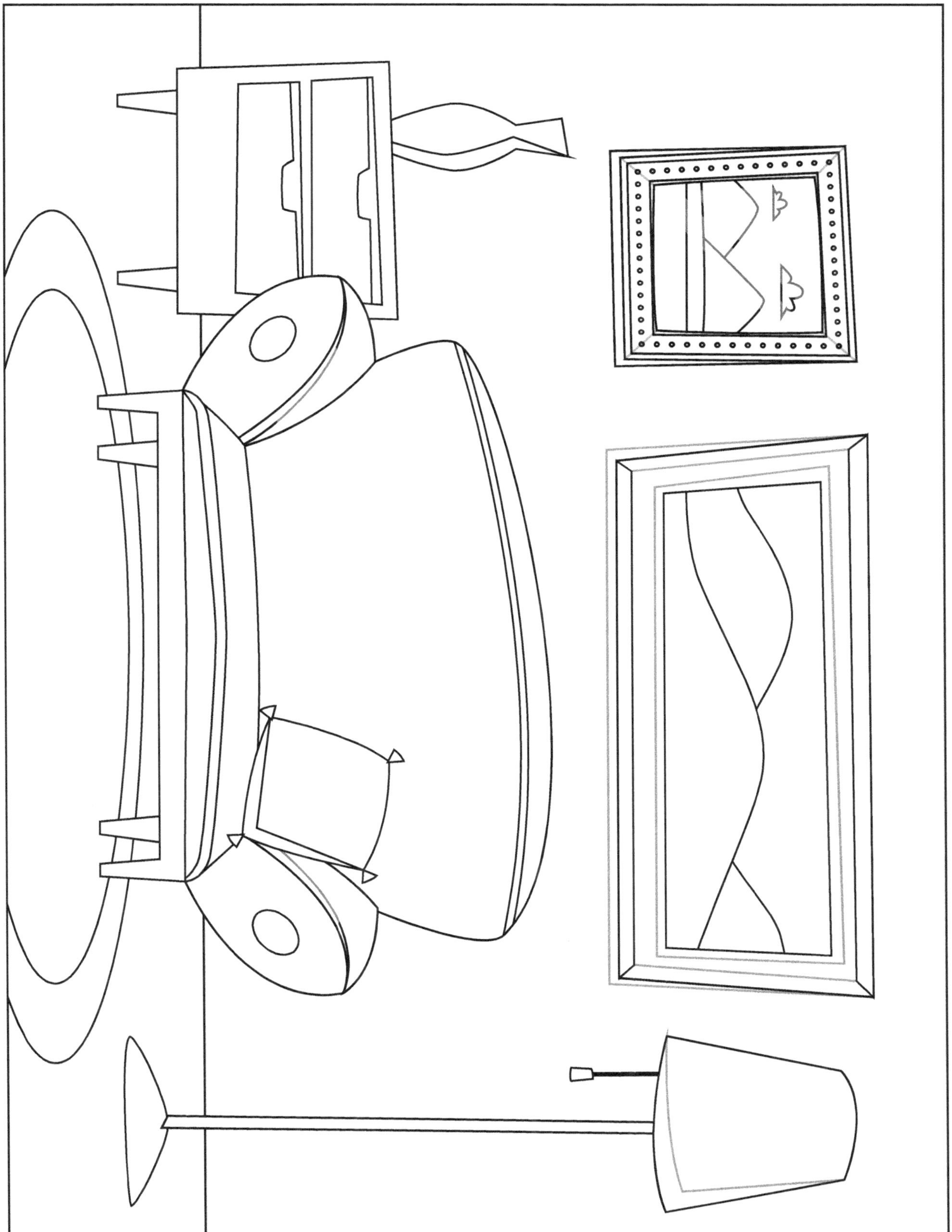

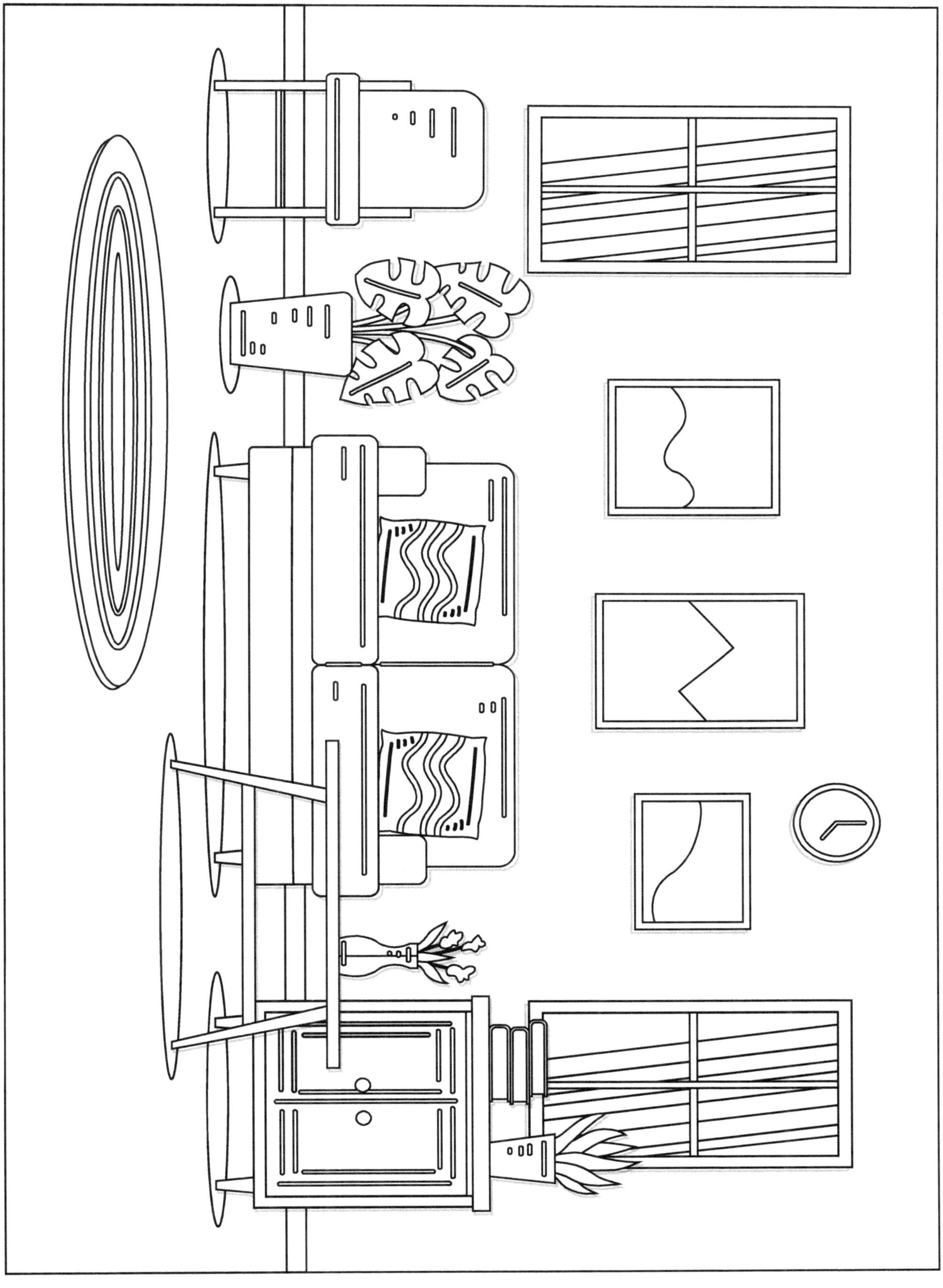

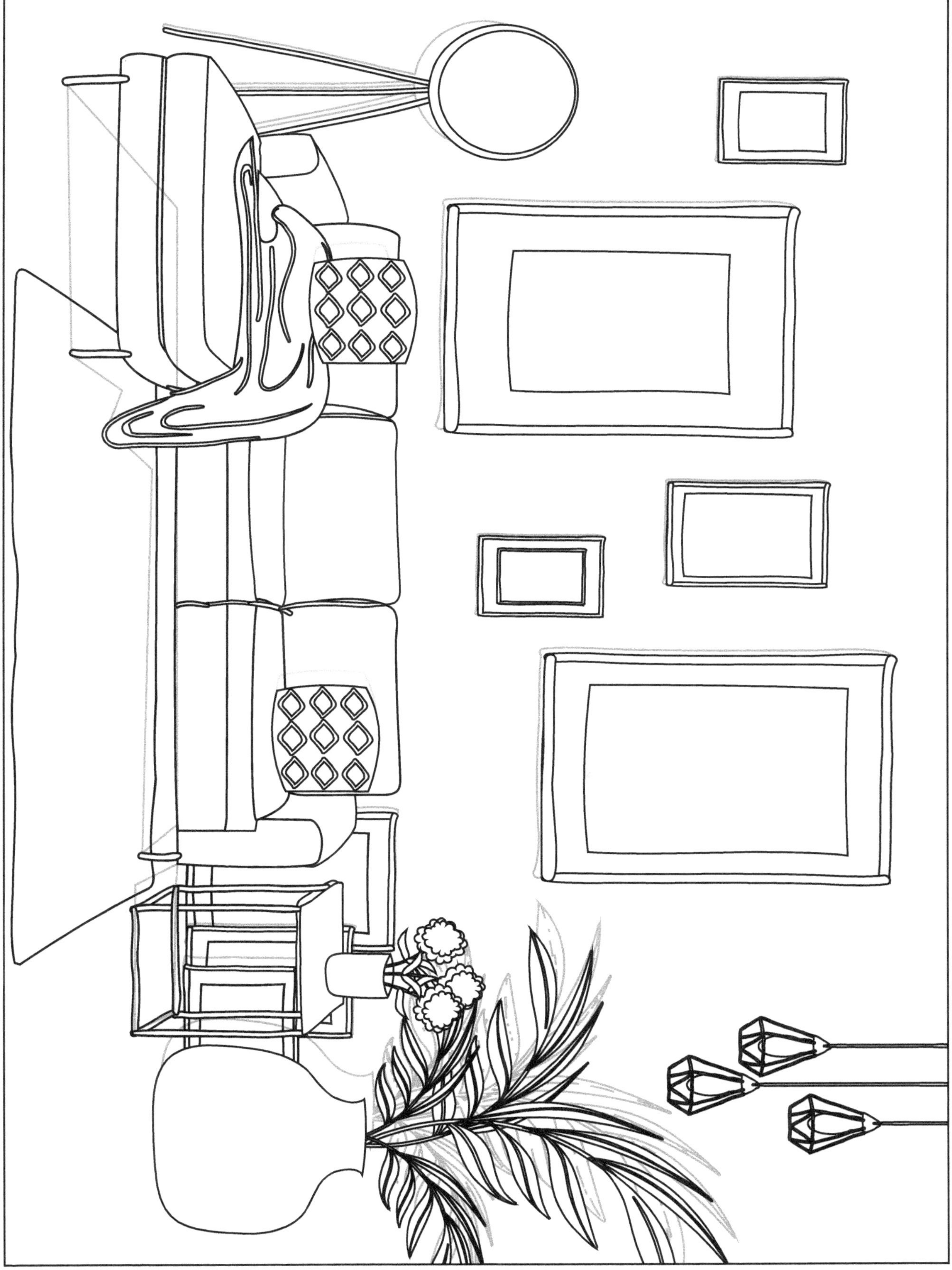

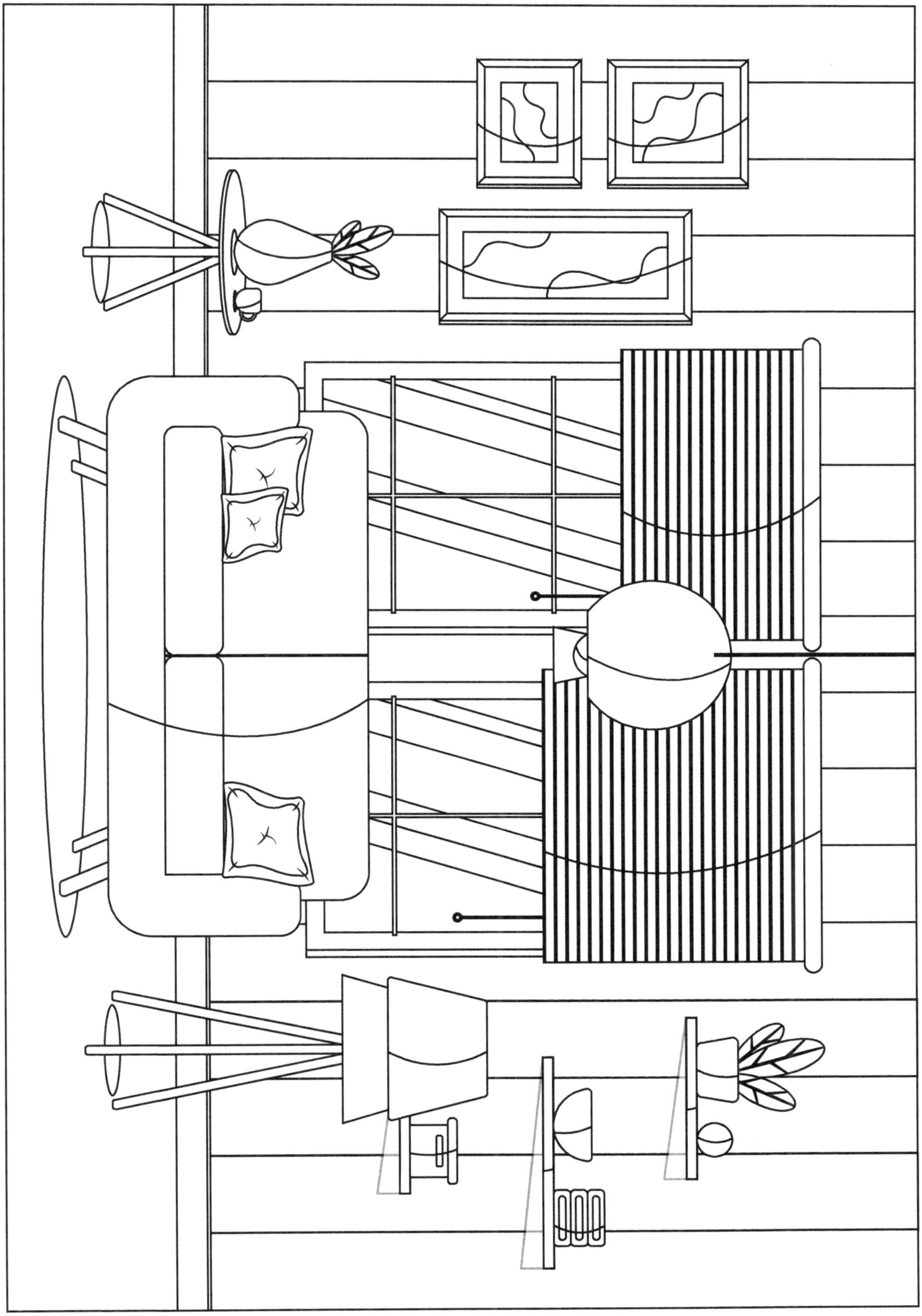

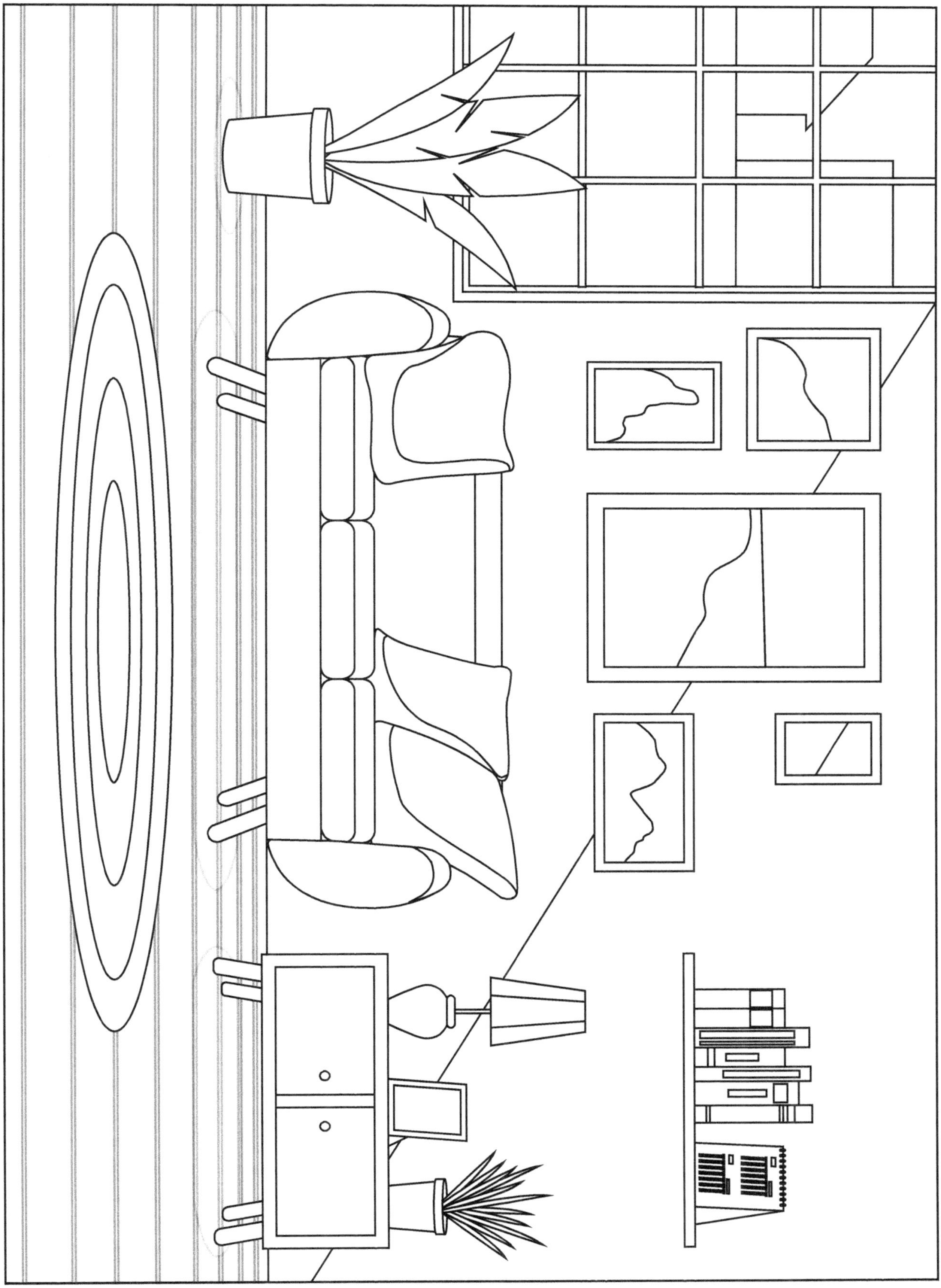

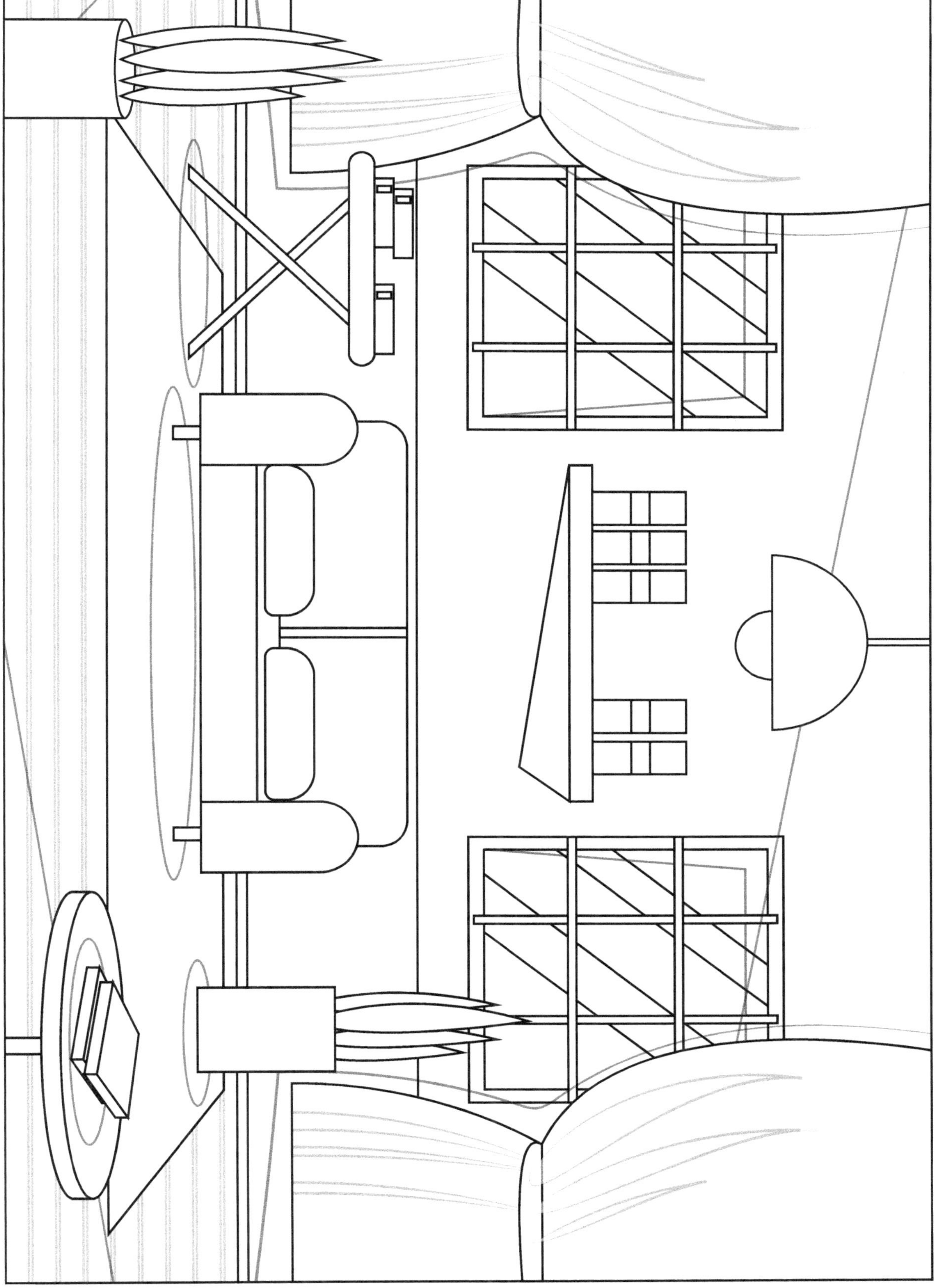

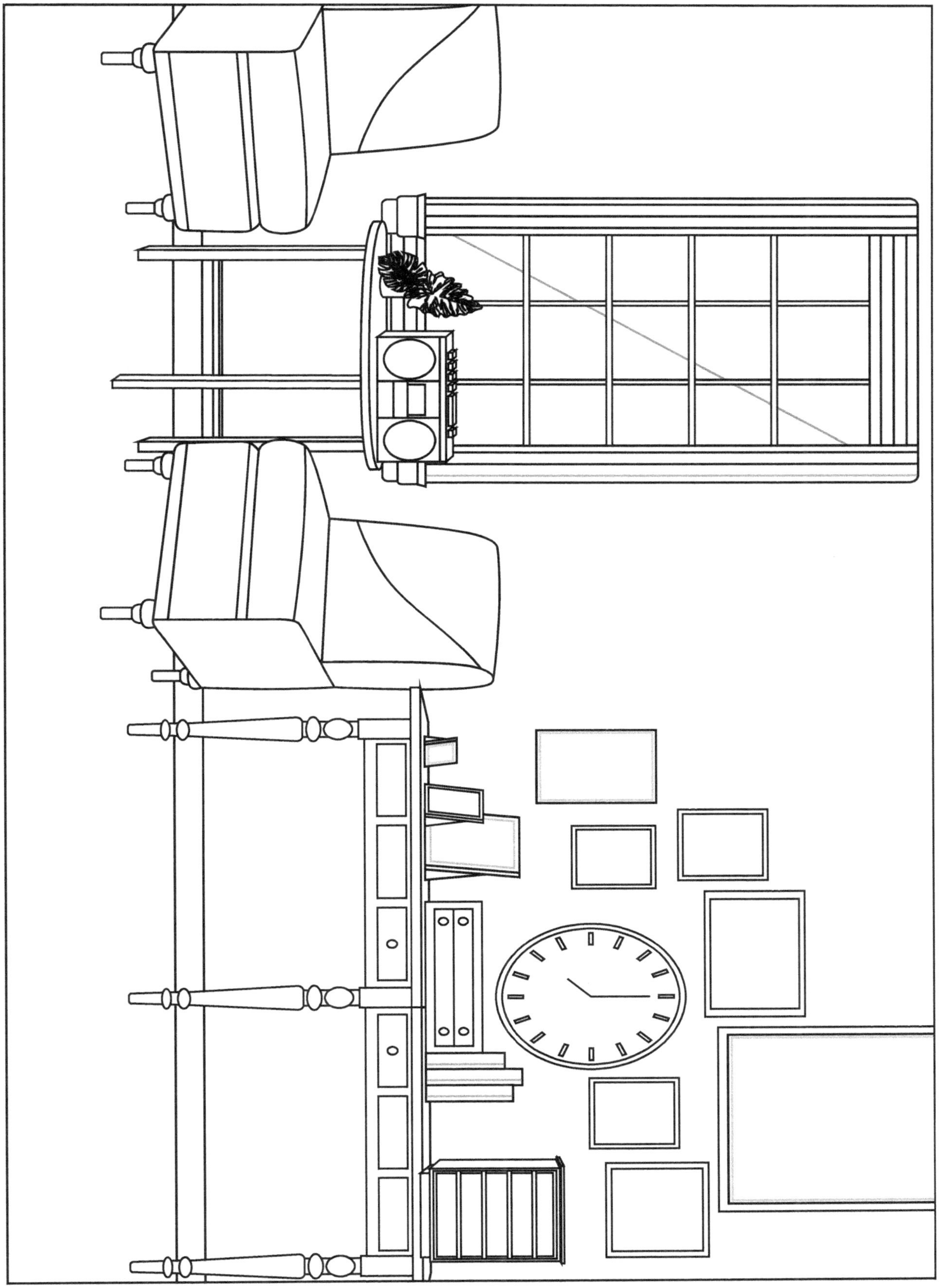

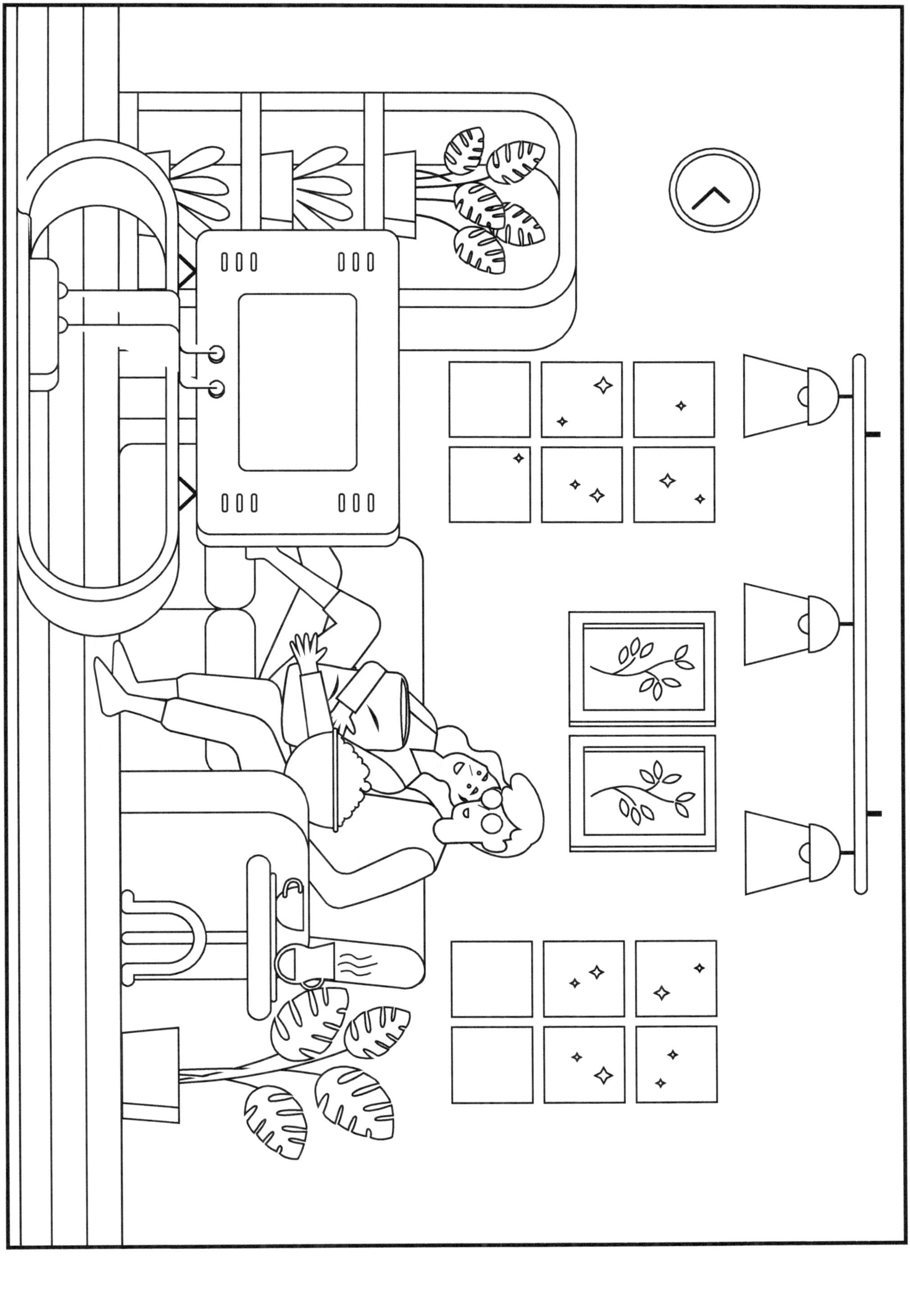

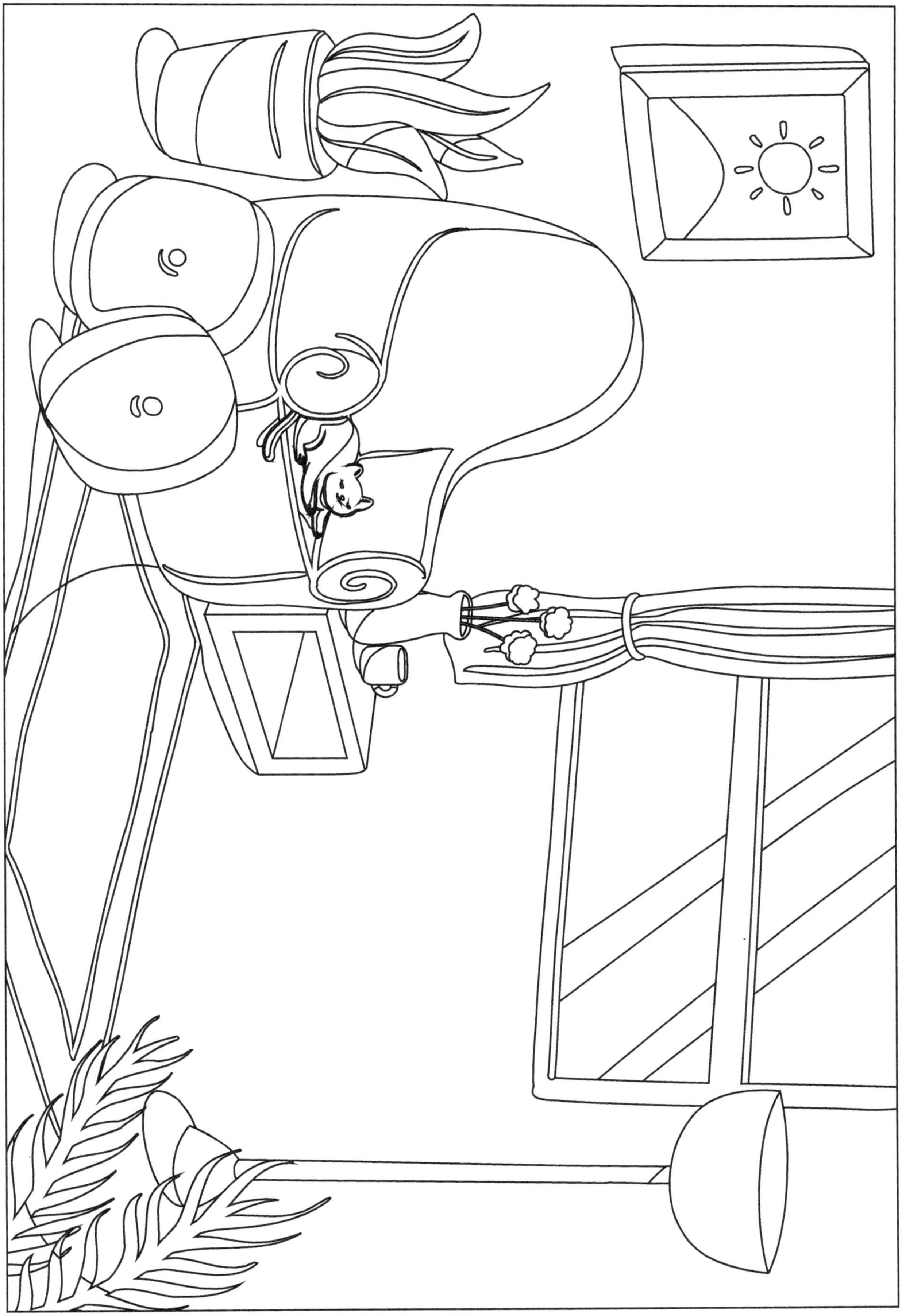

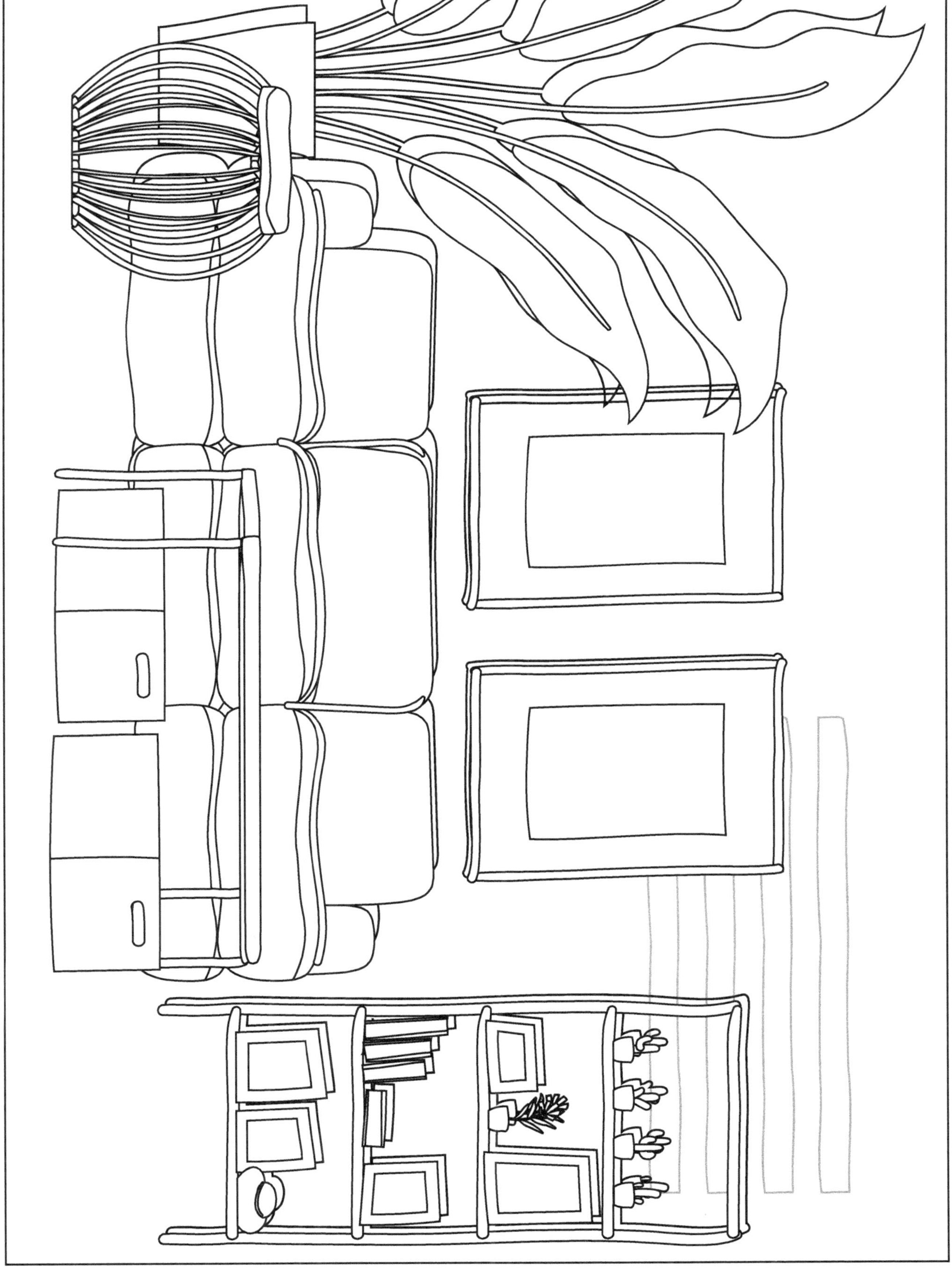

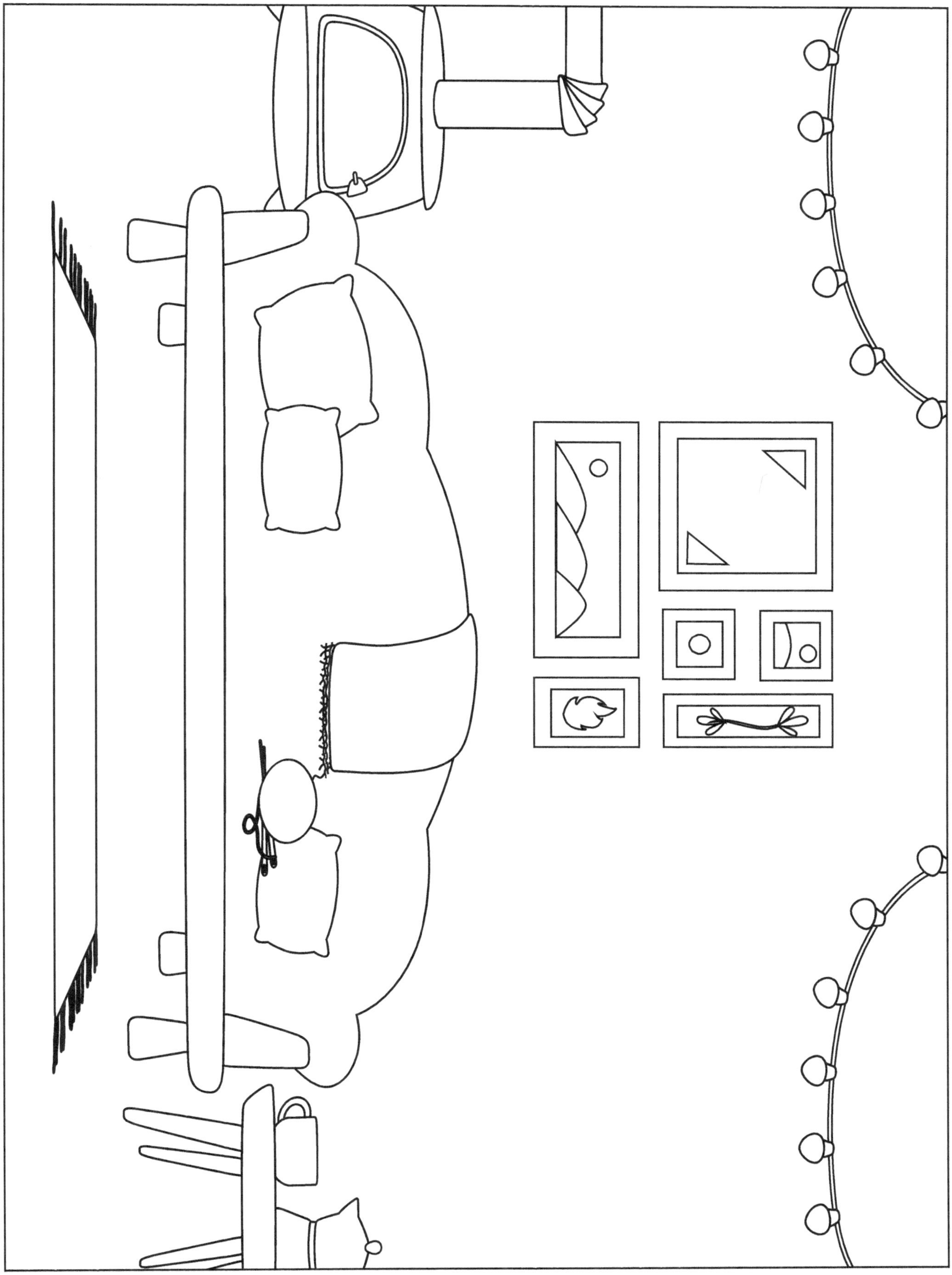

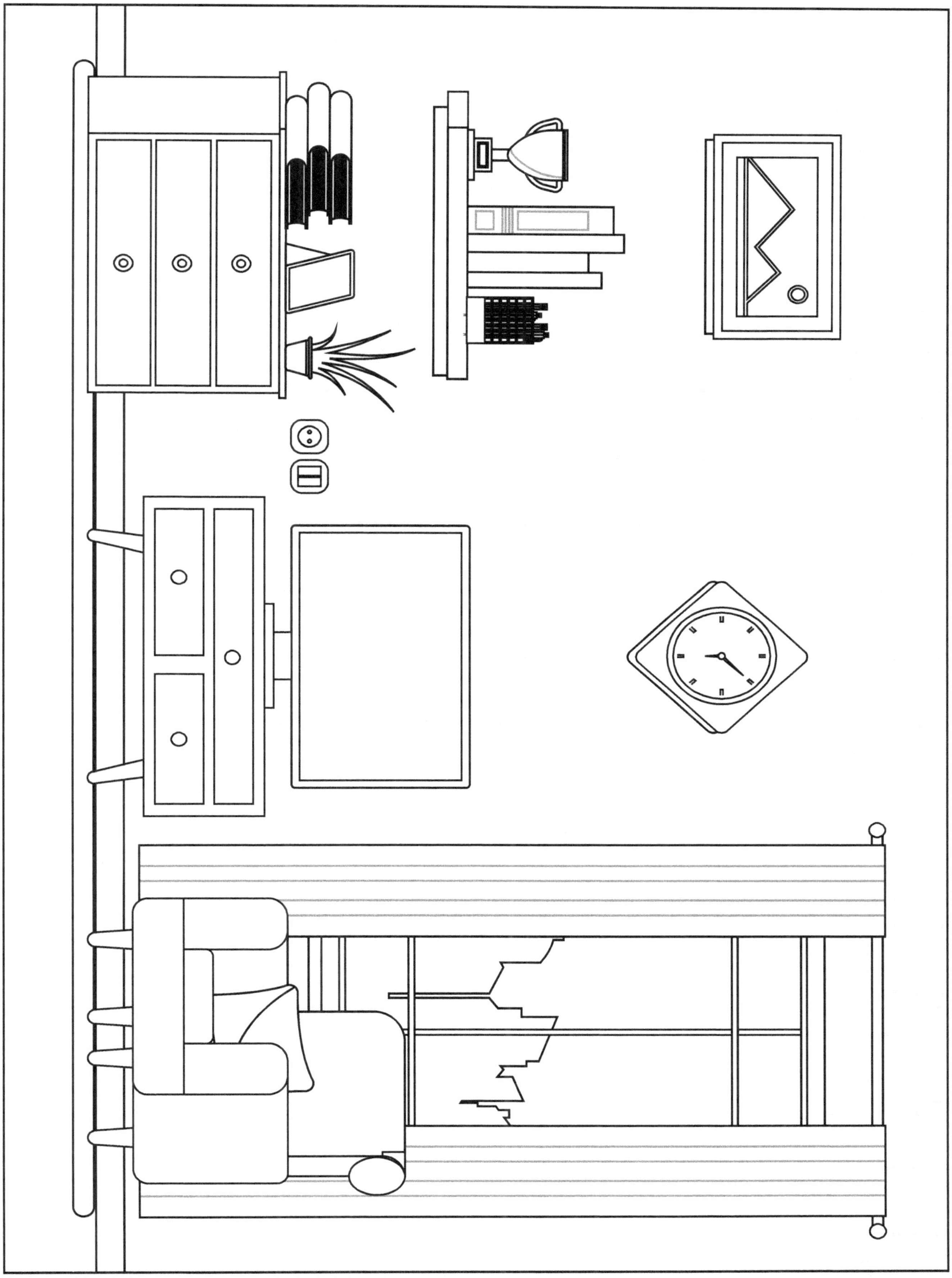

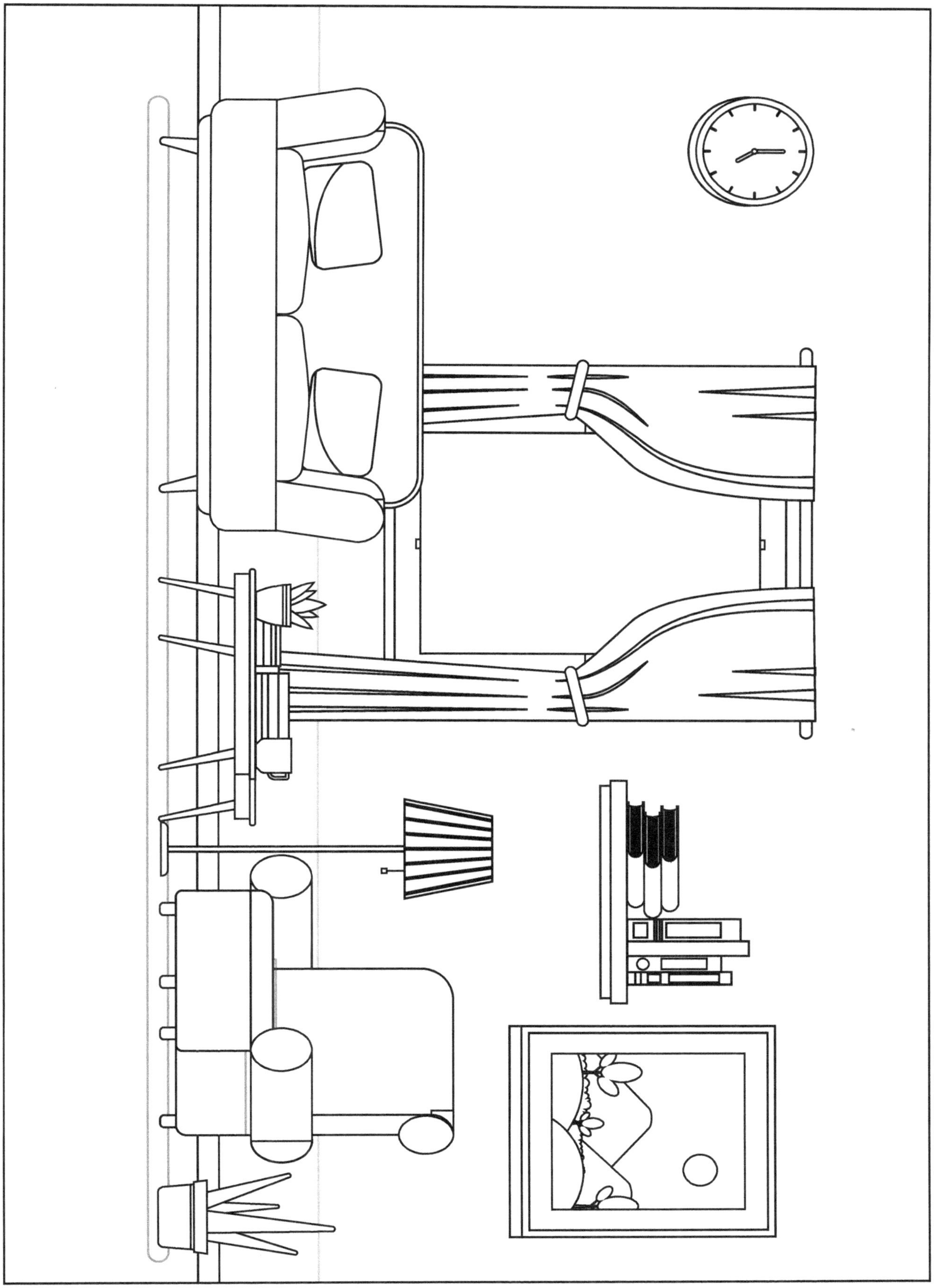

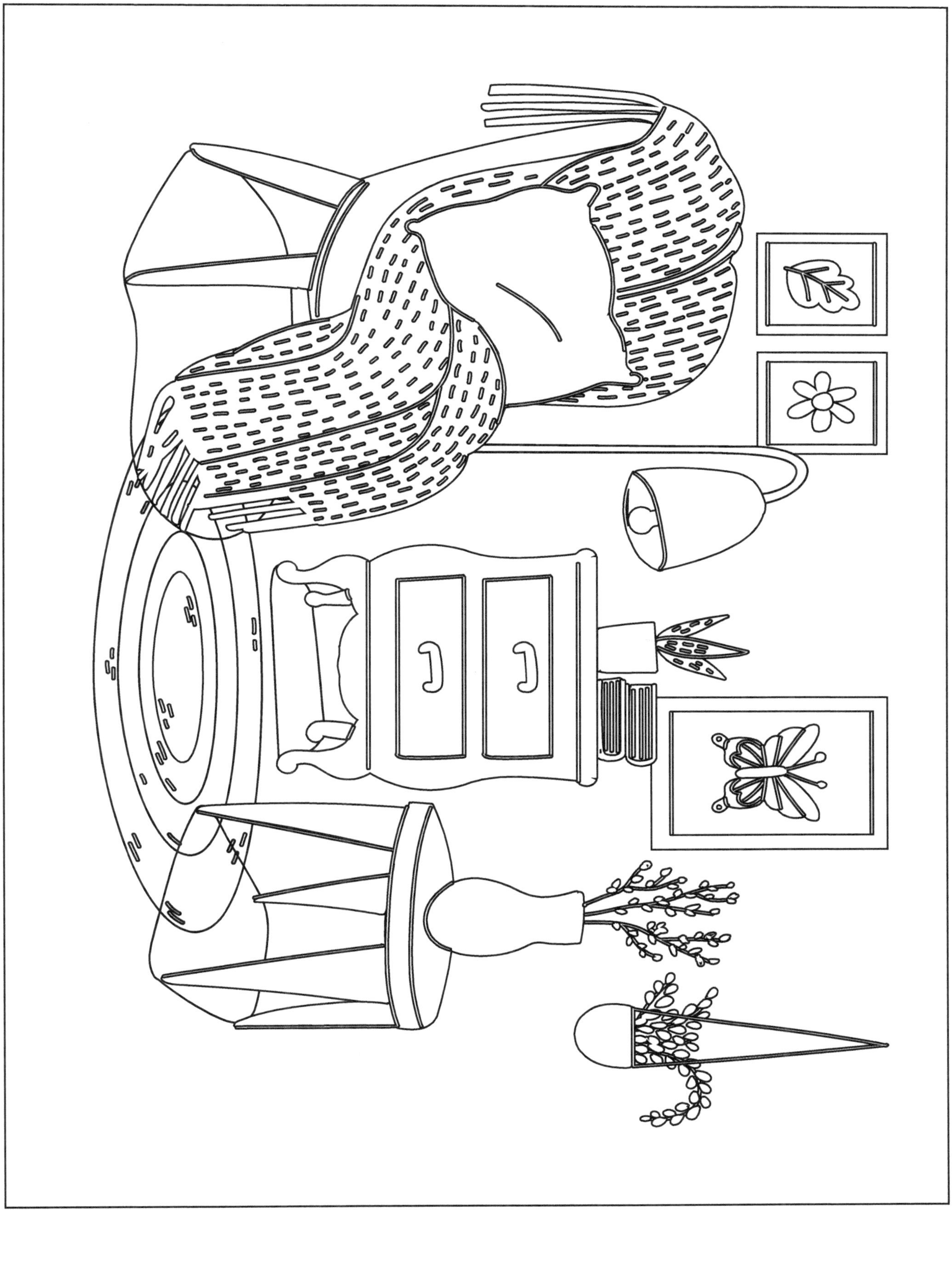

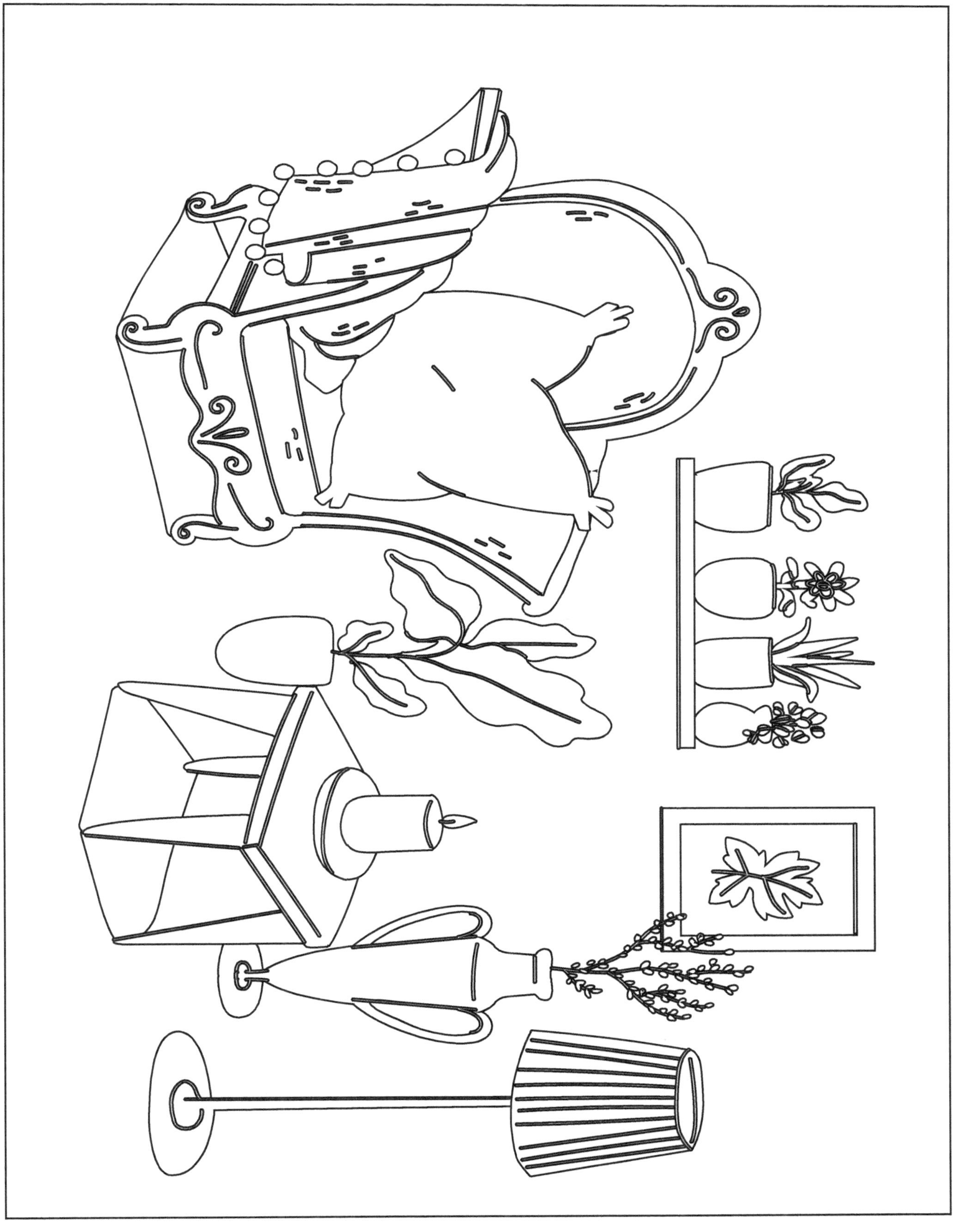

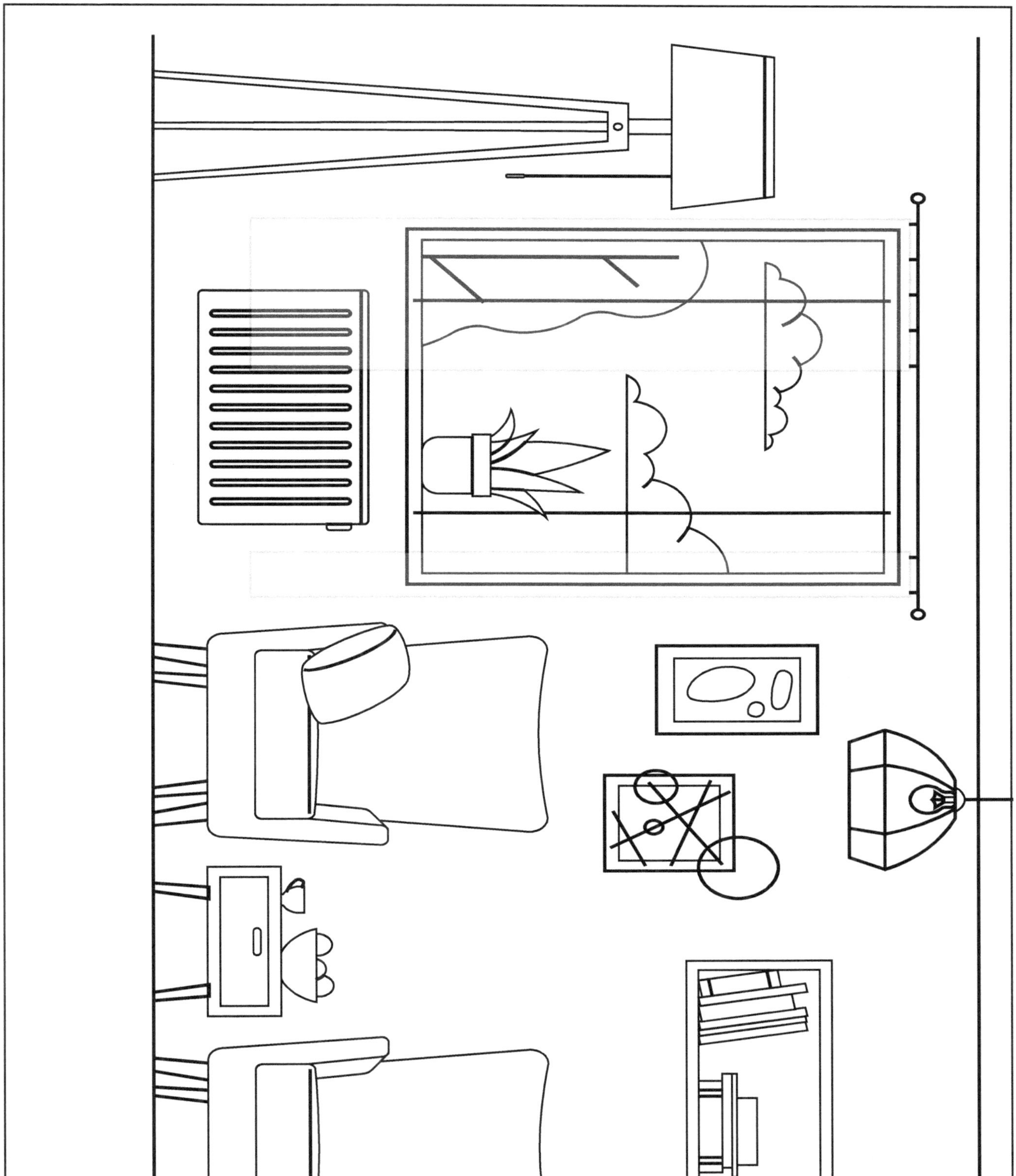

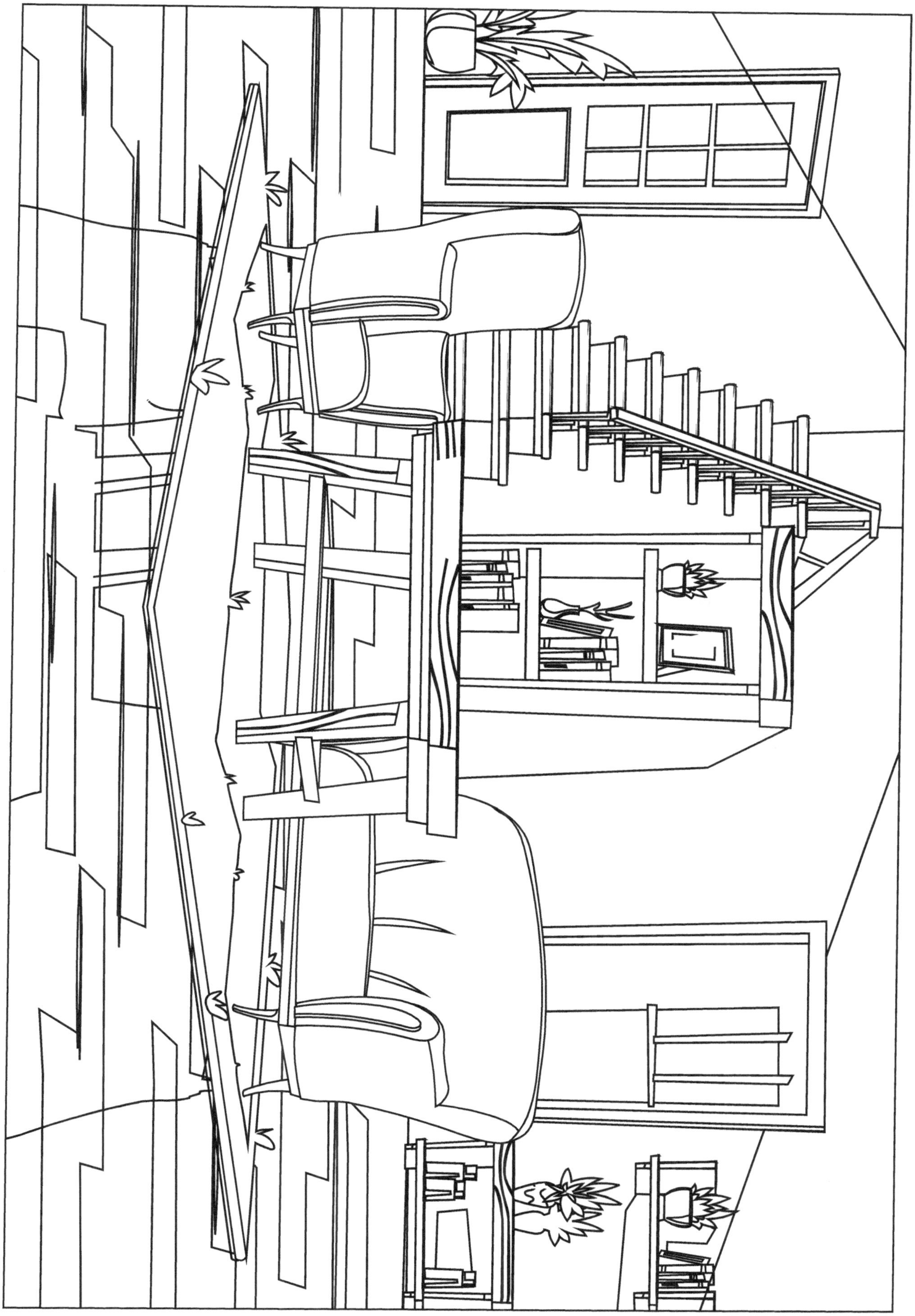

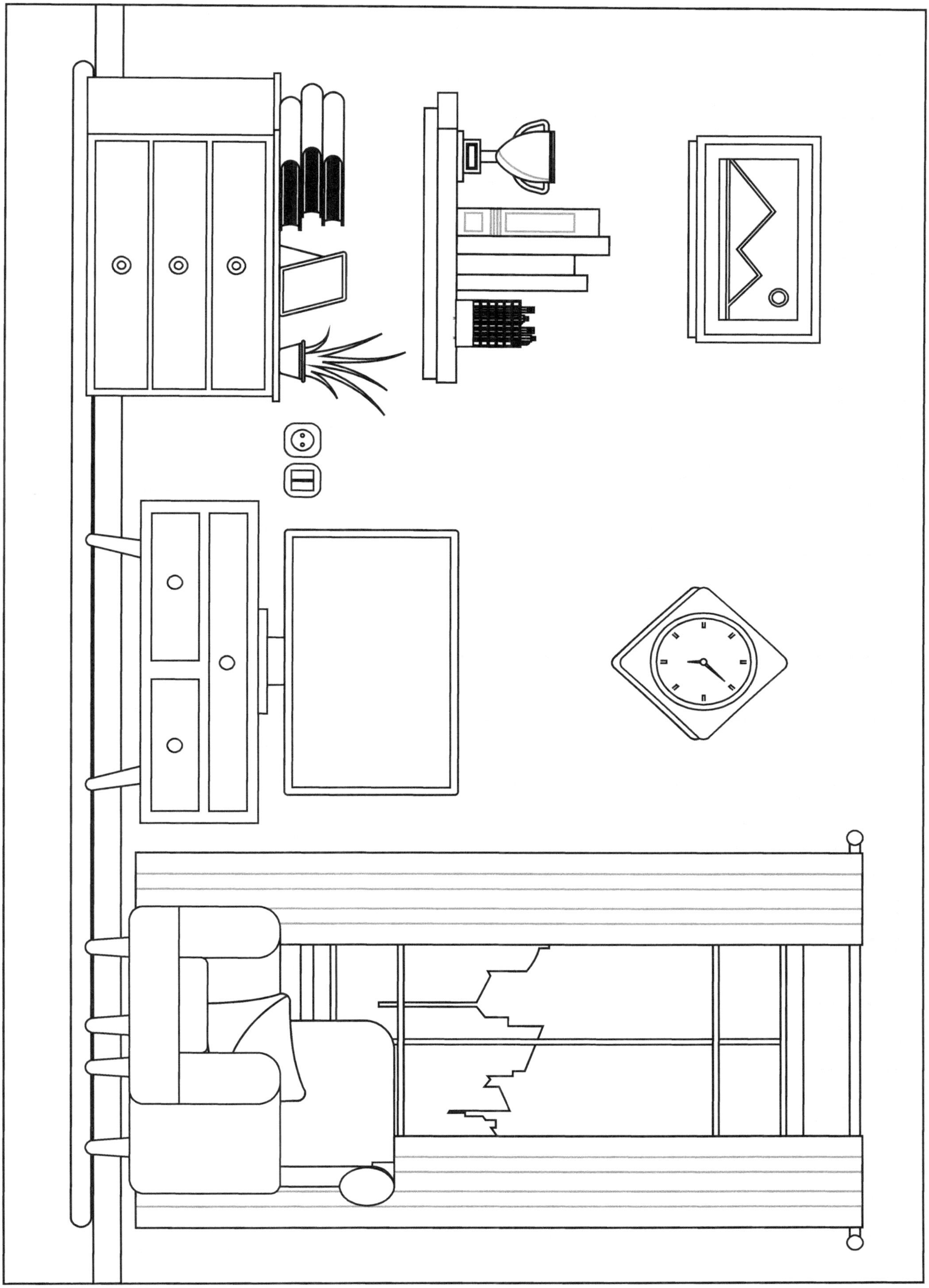

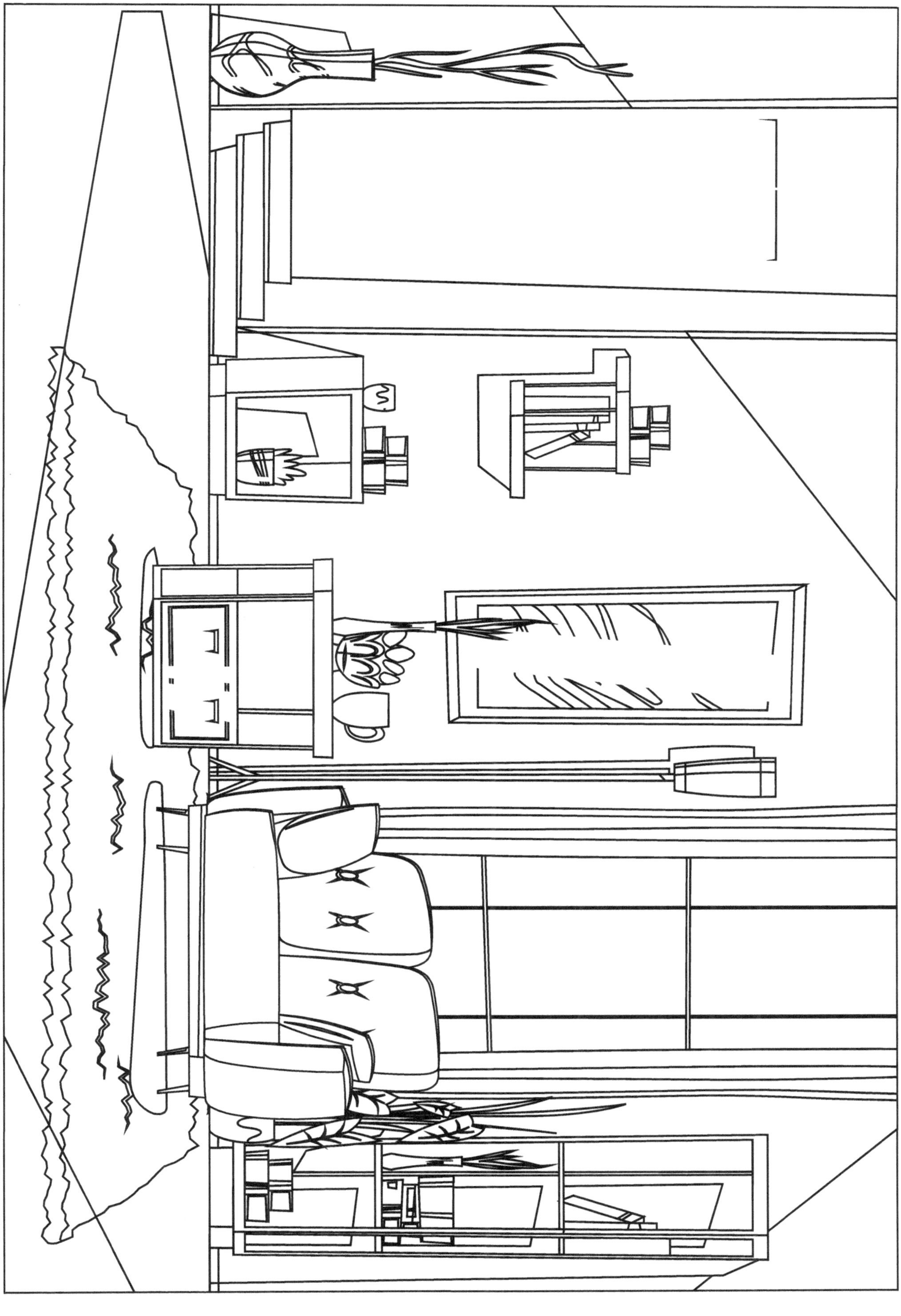

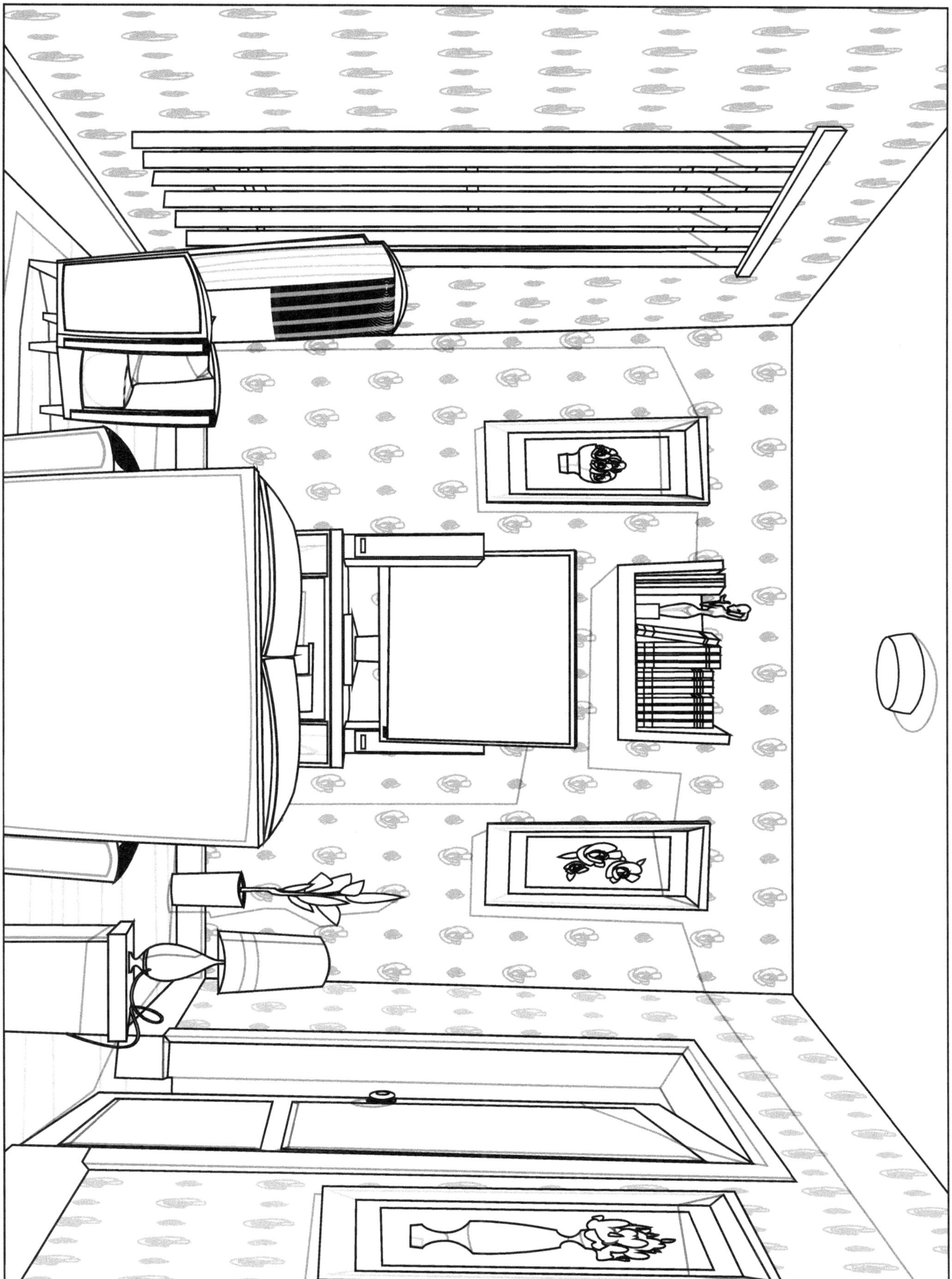

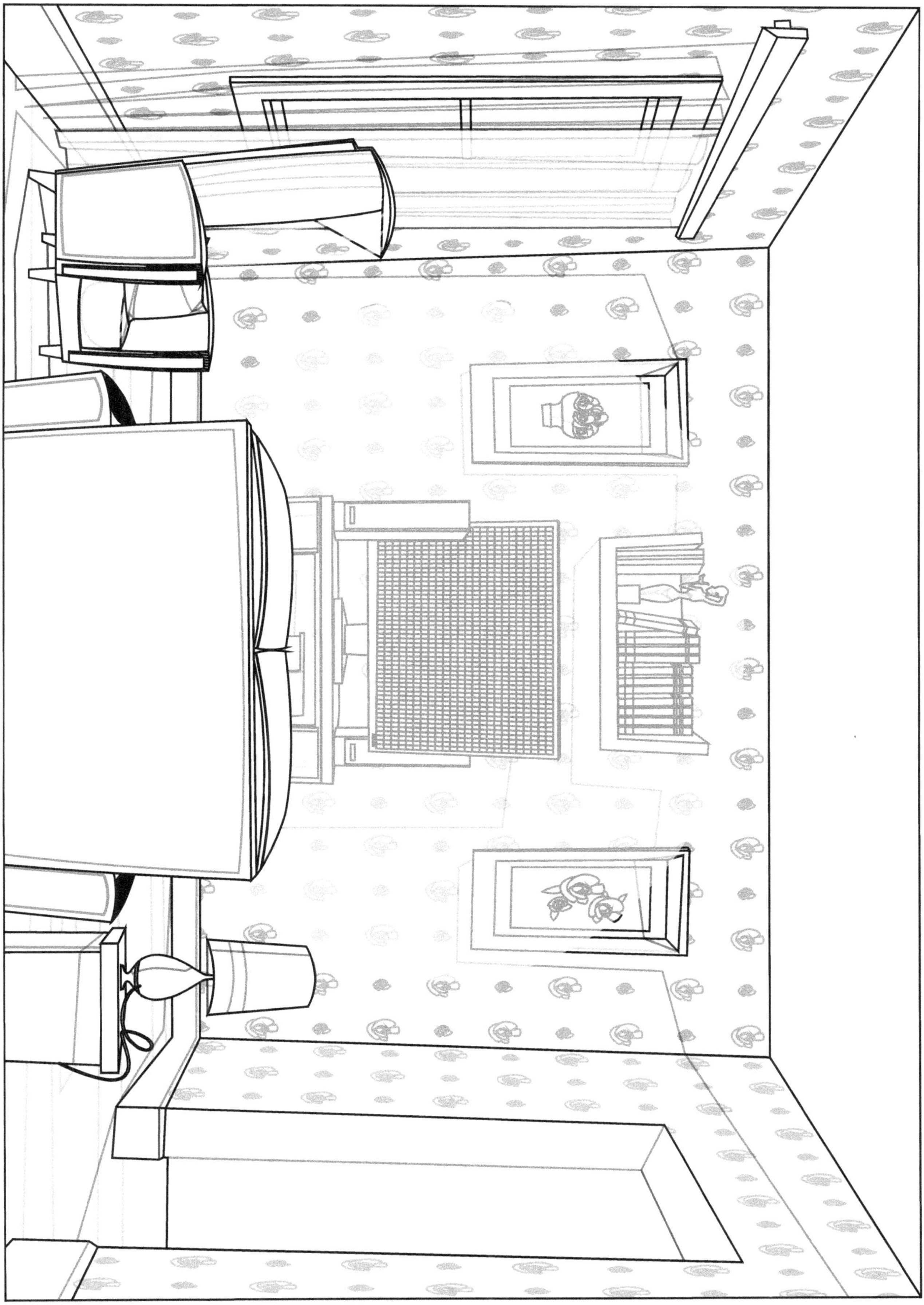

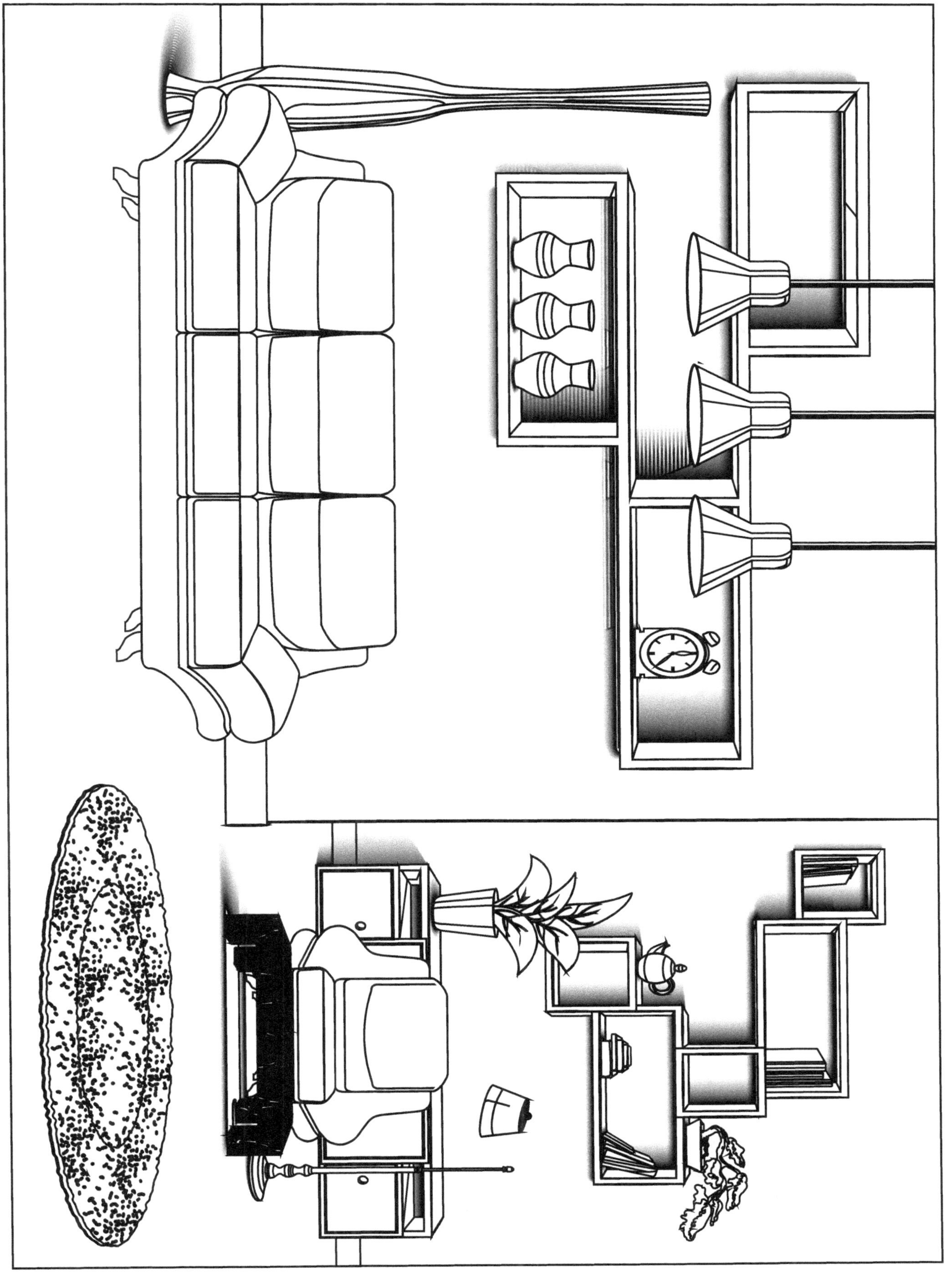

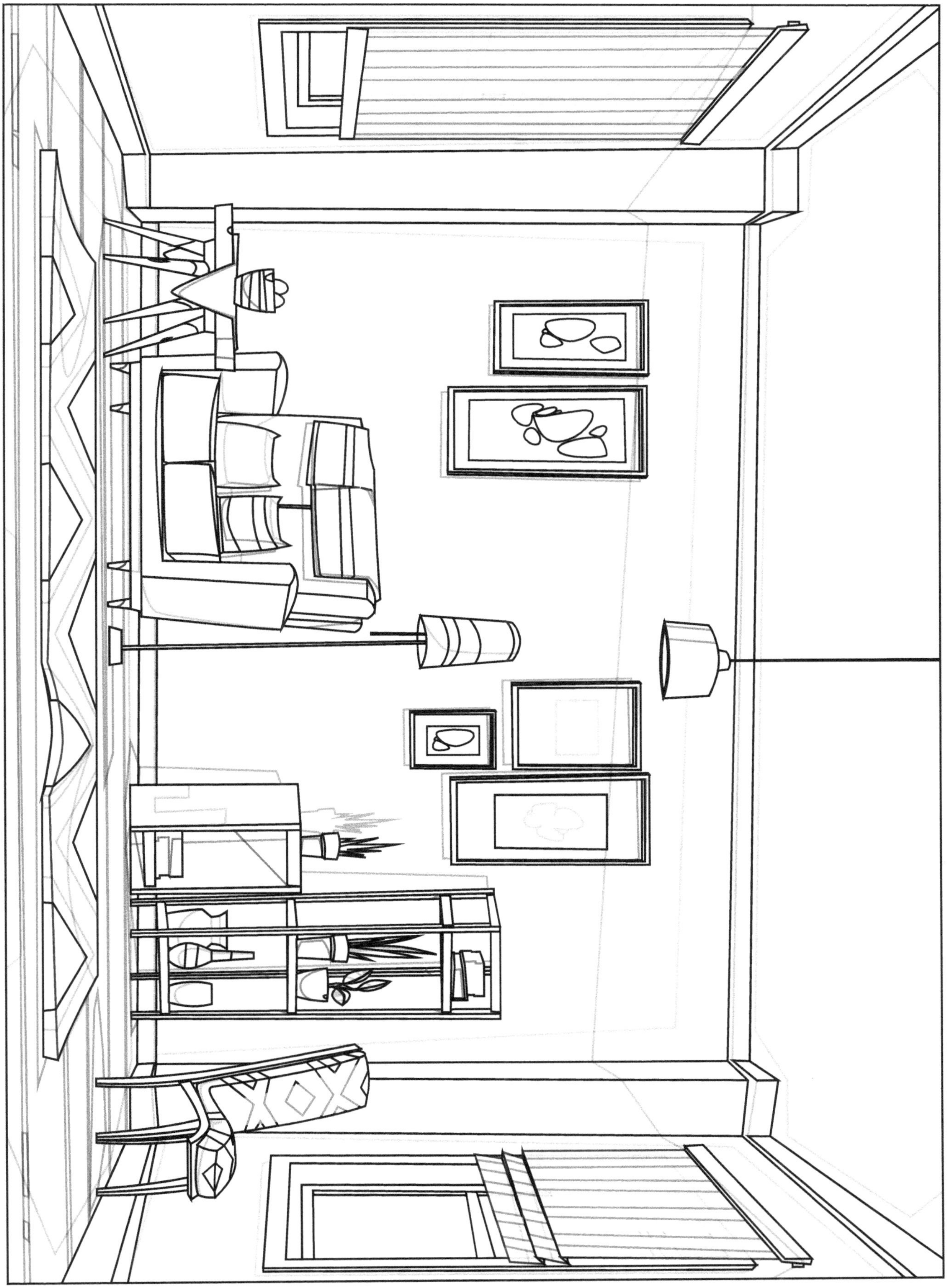

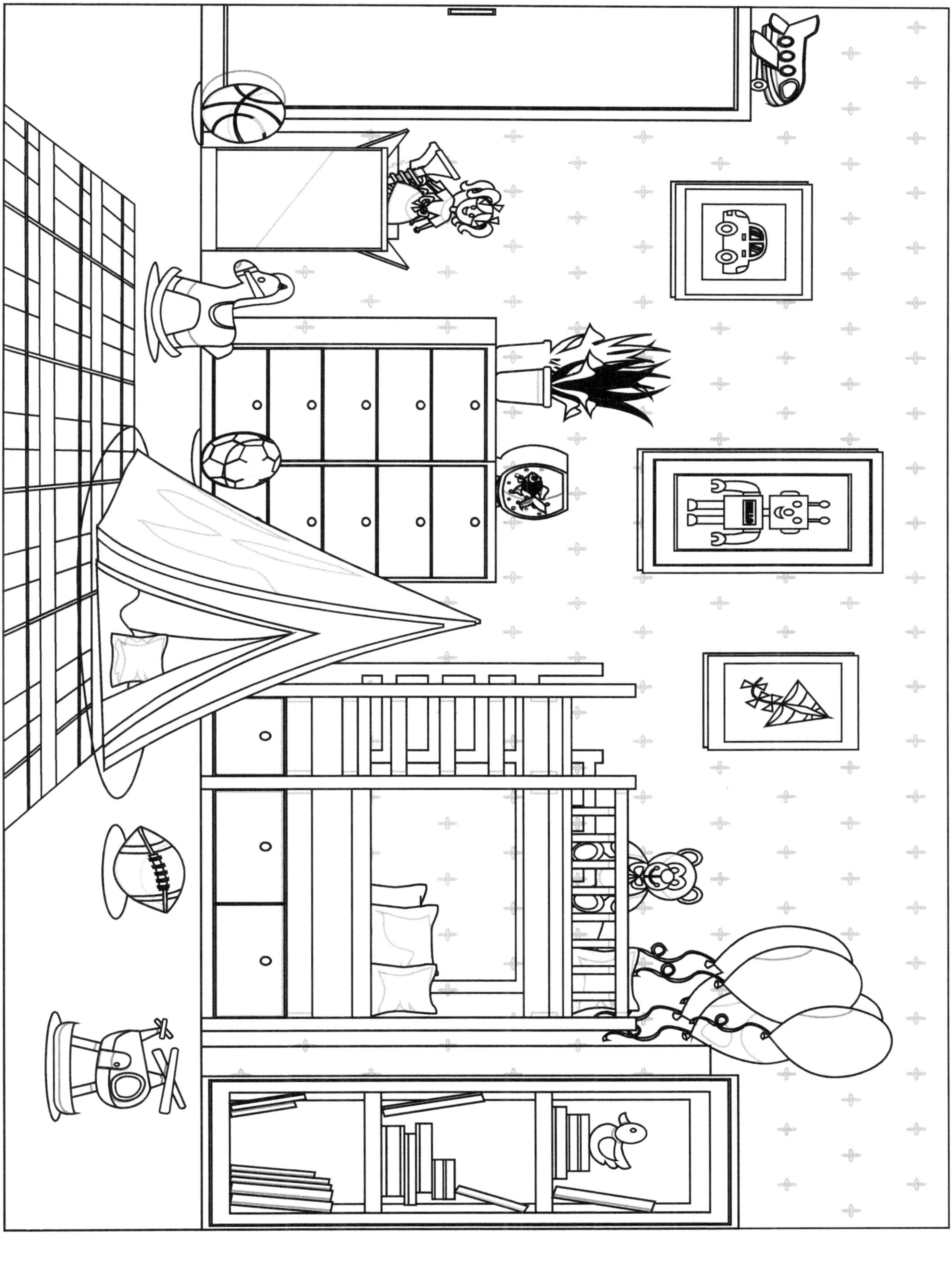

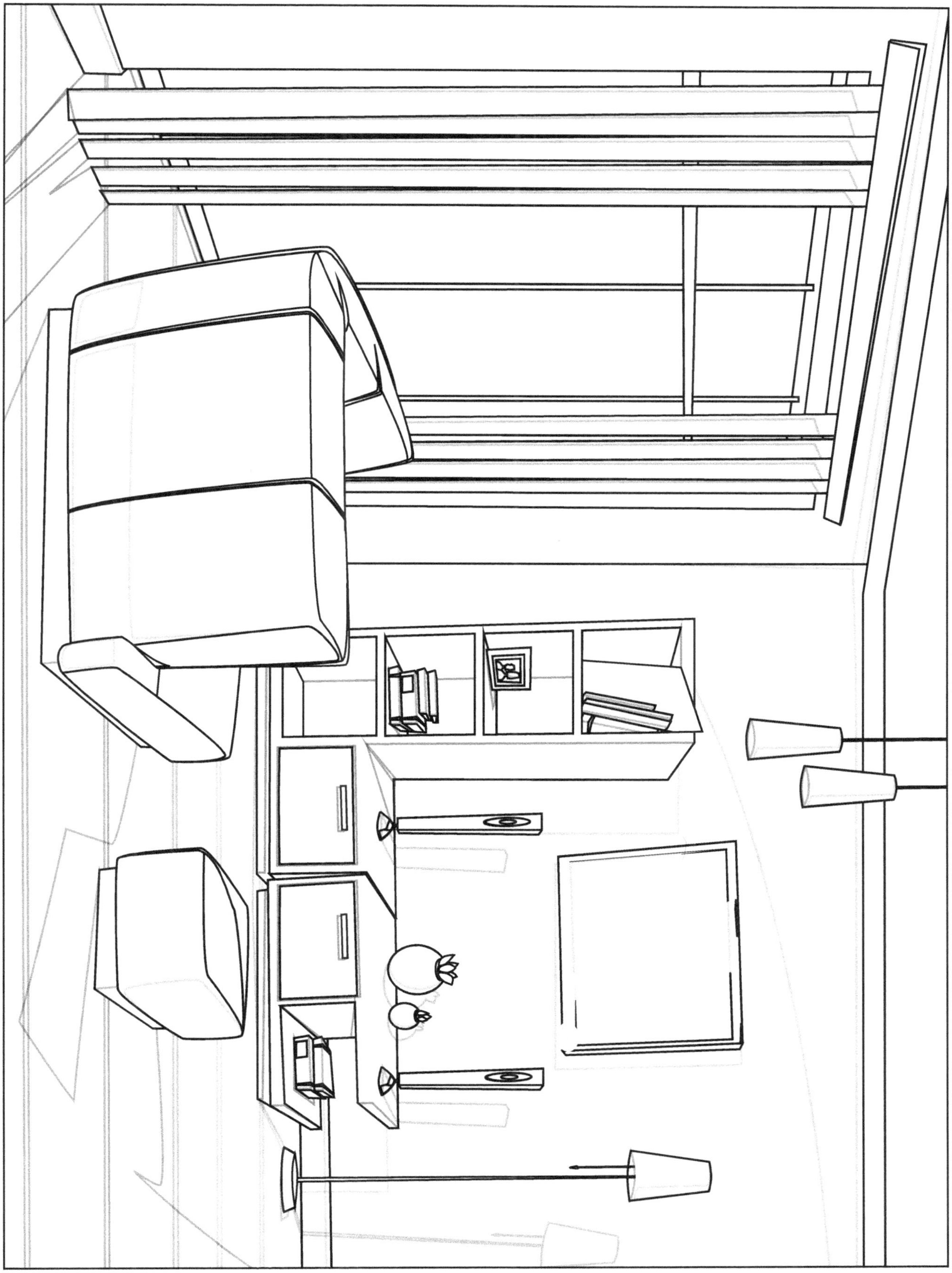

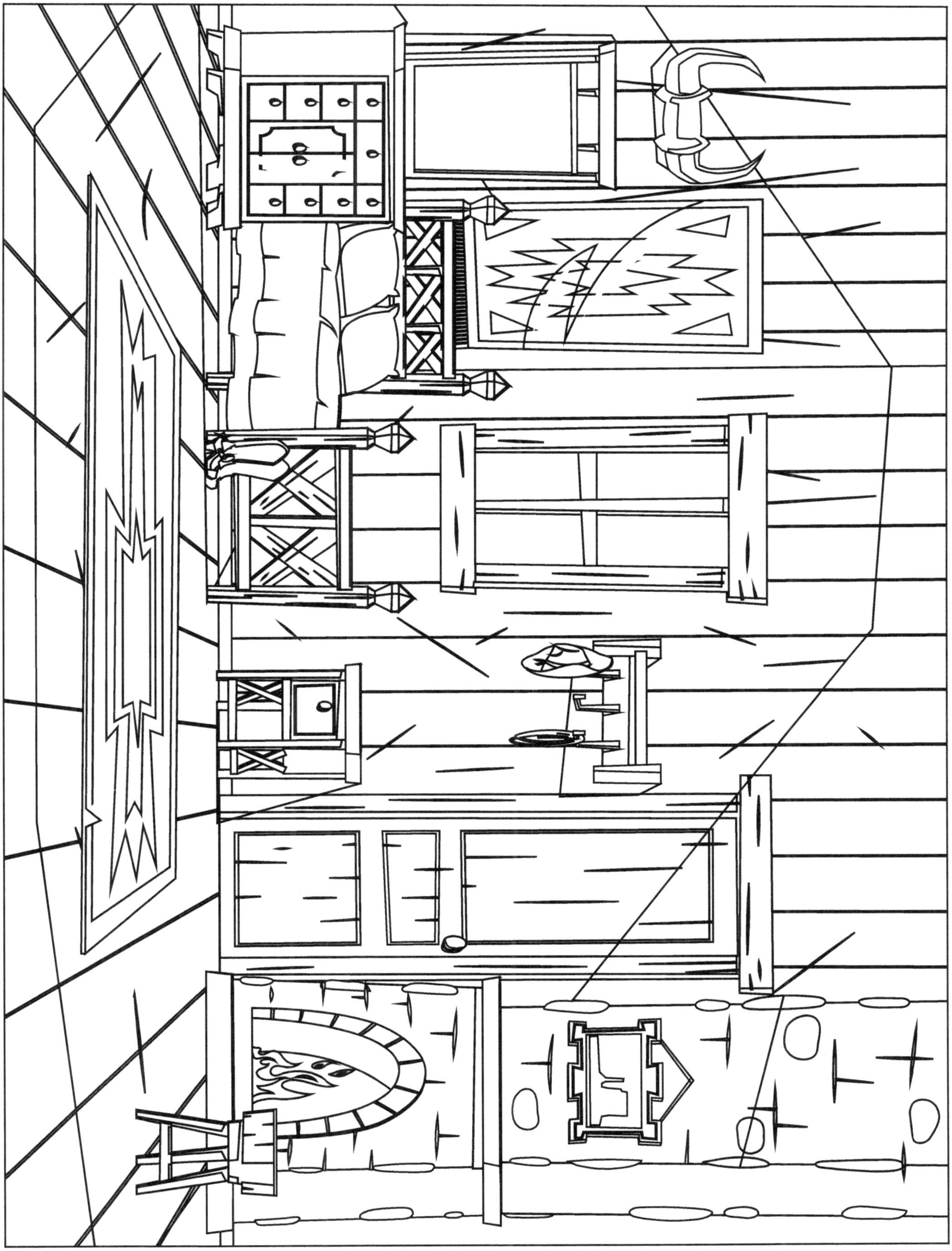

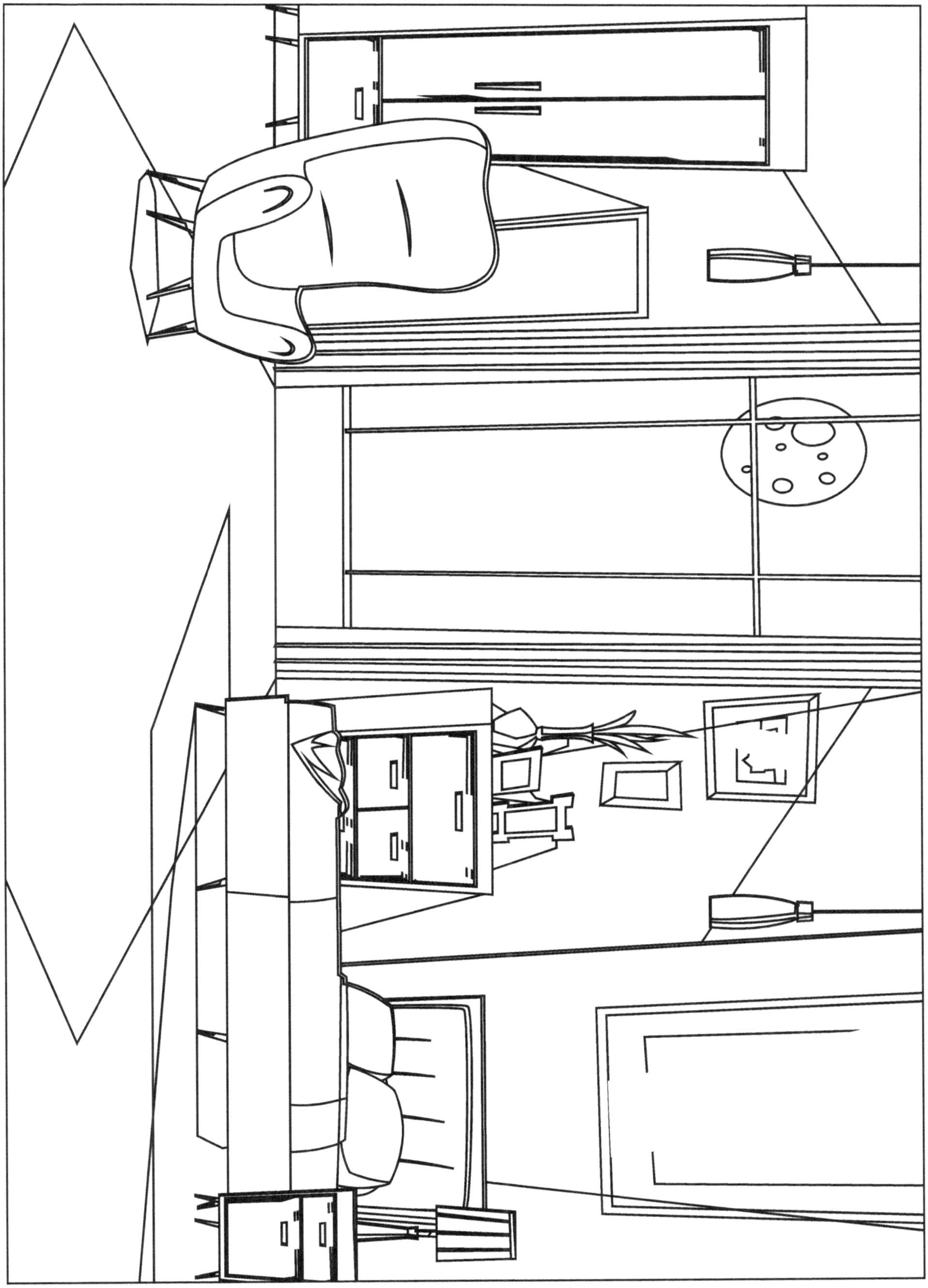

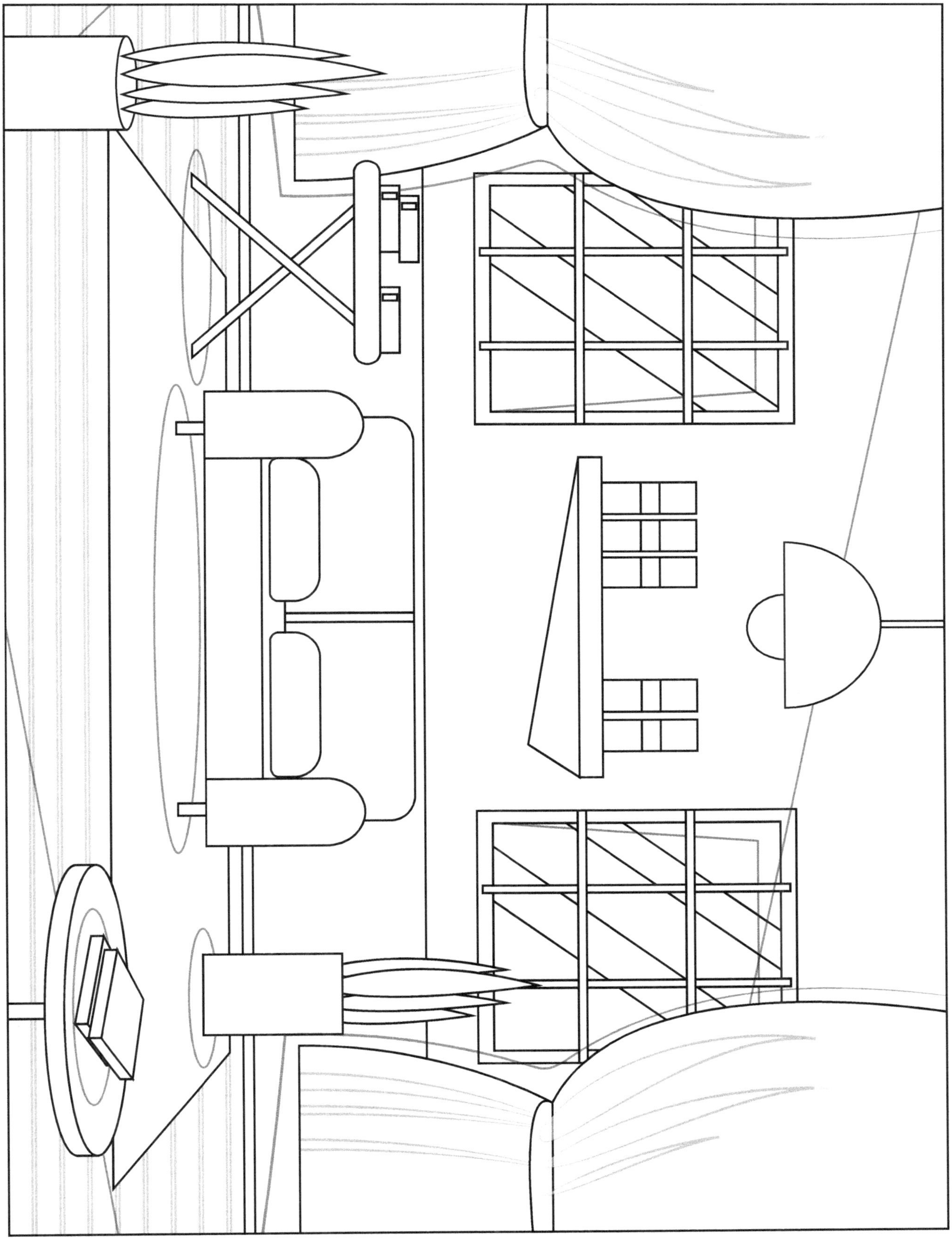

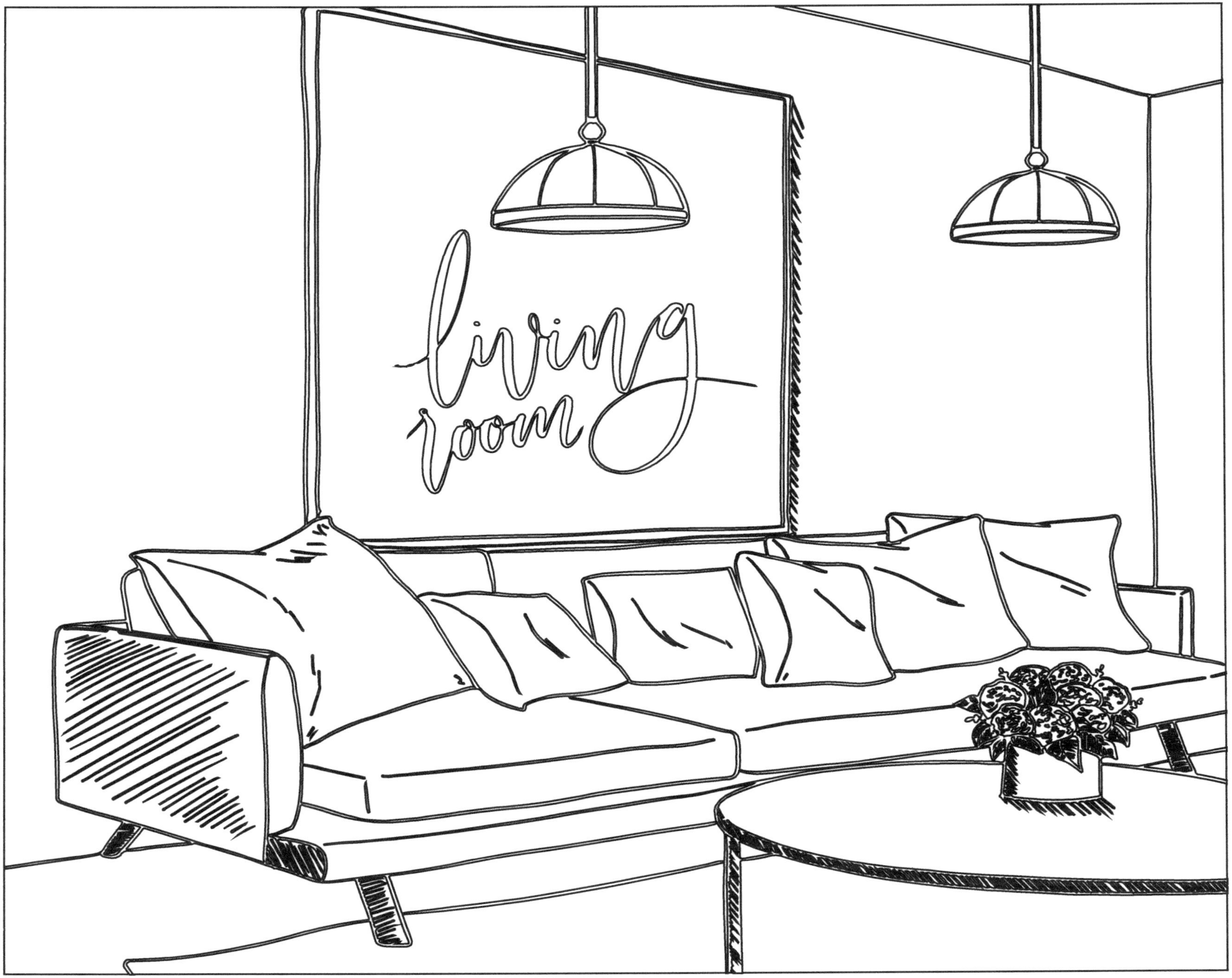
Living room

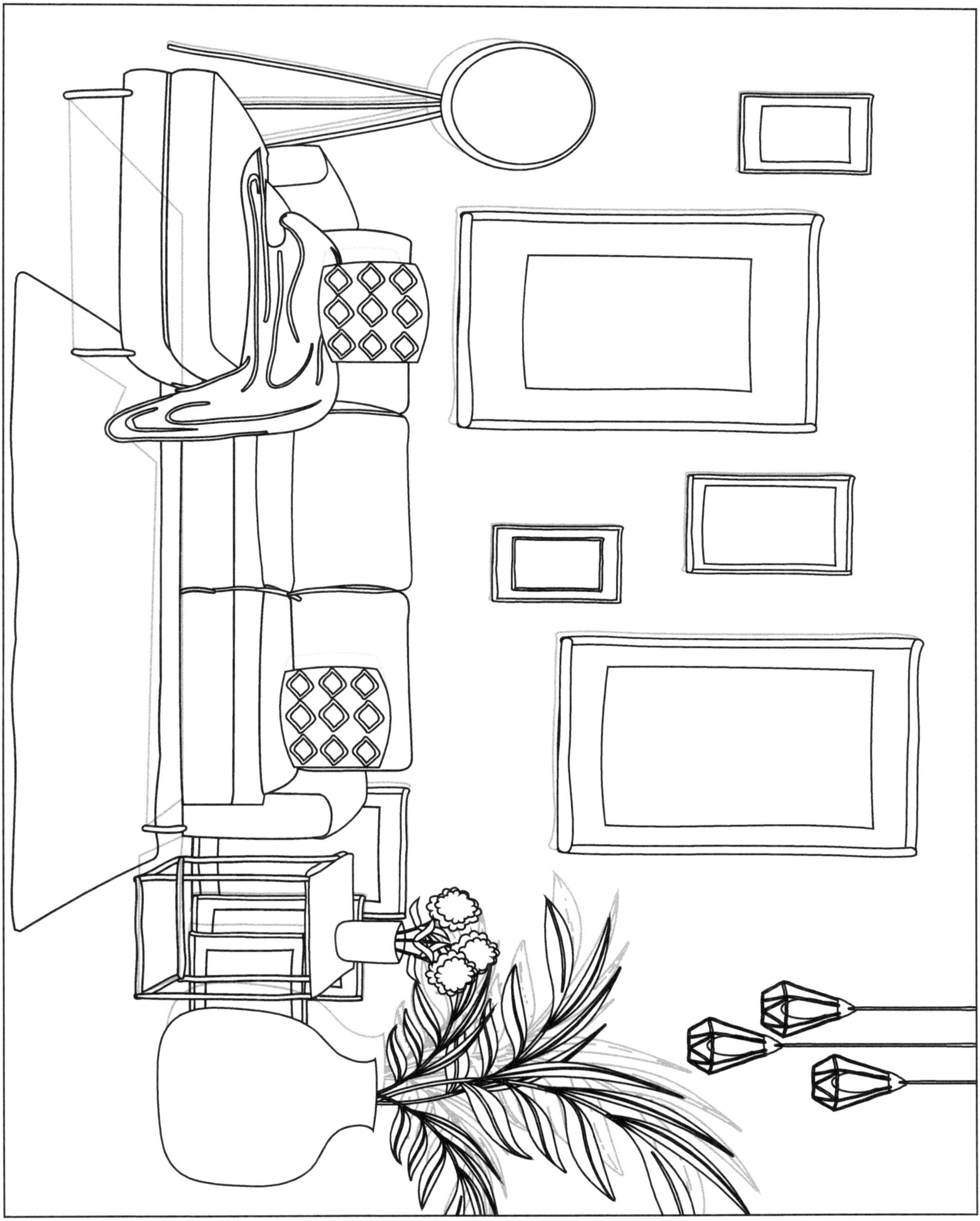

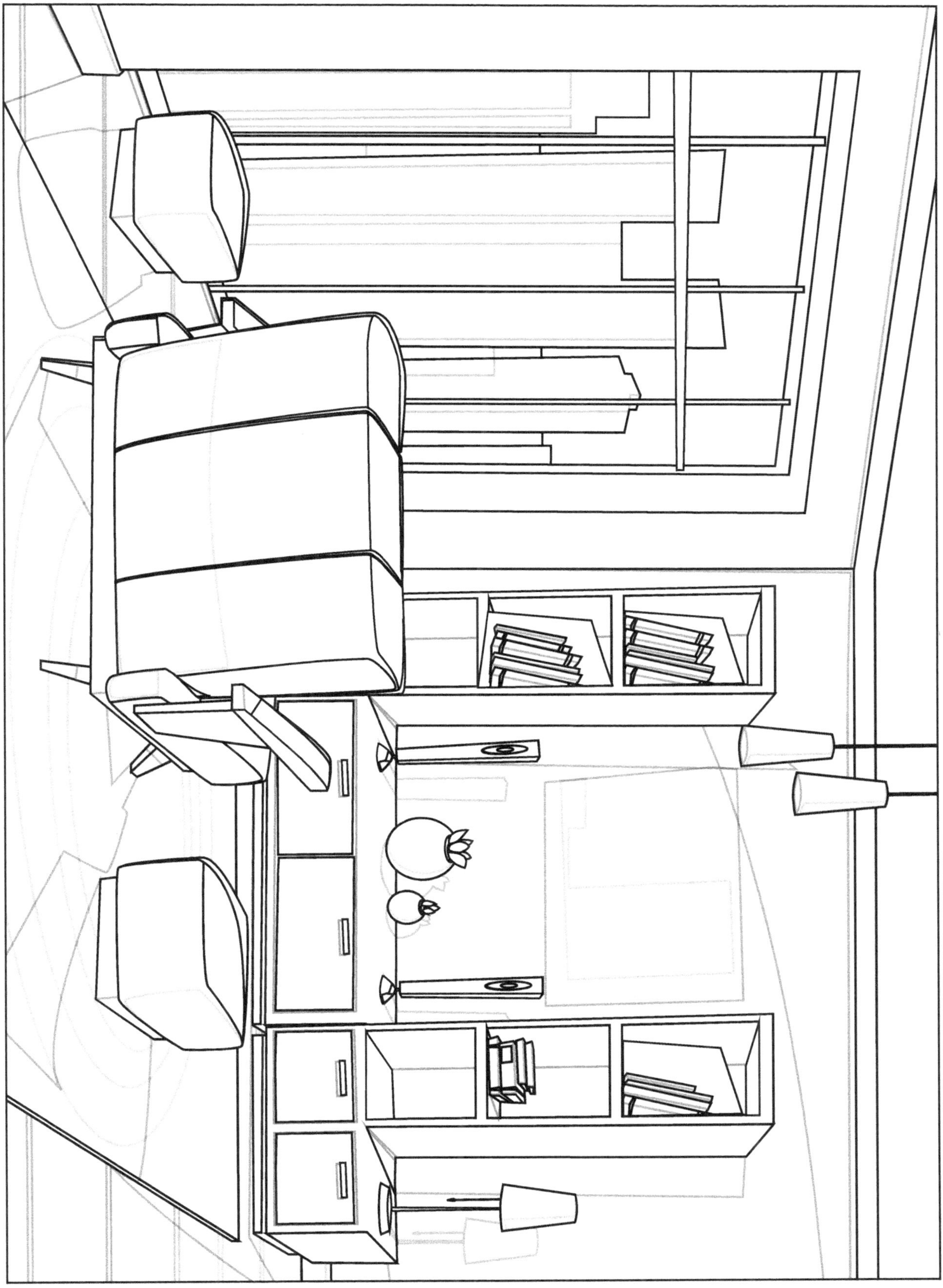

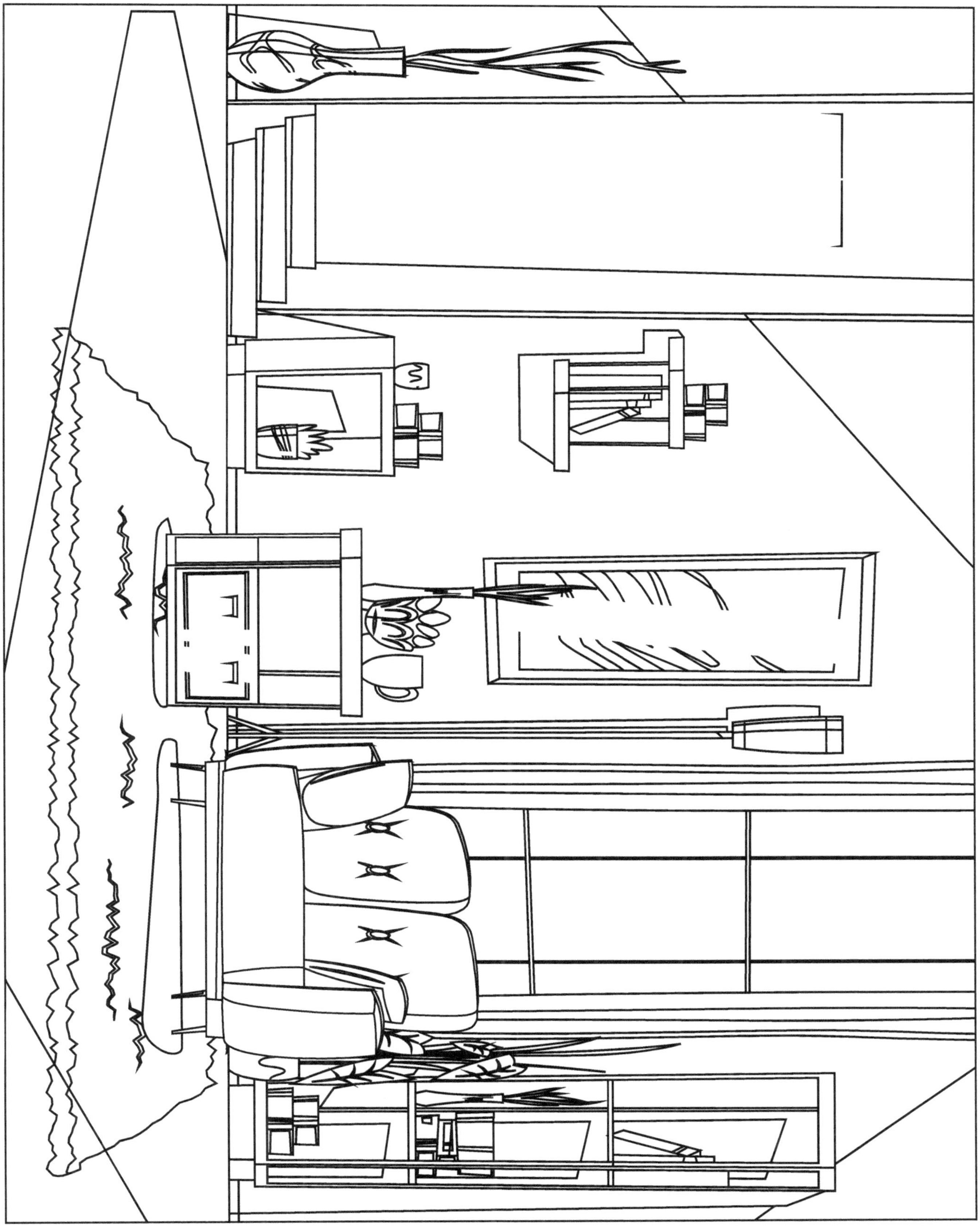

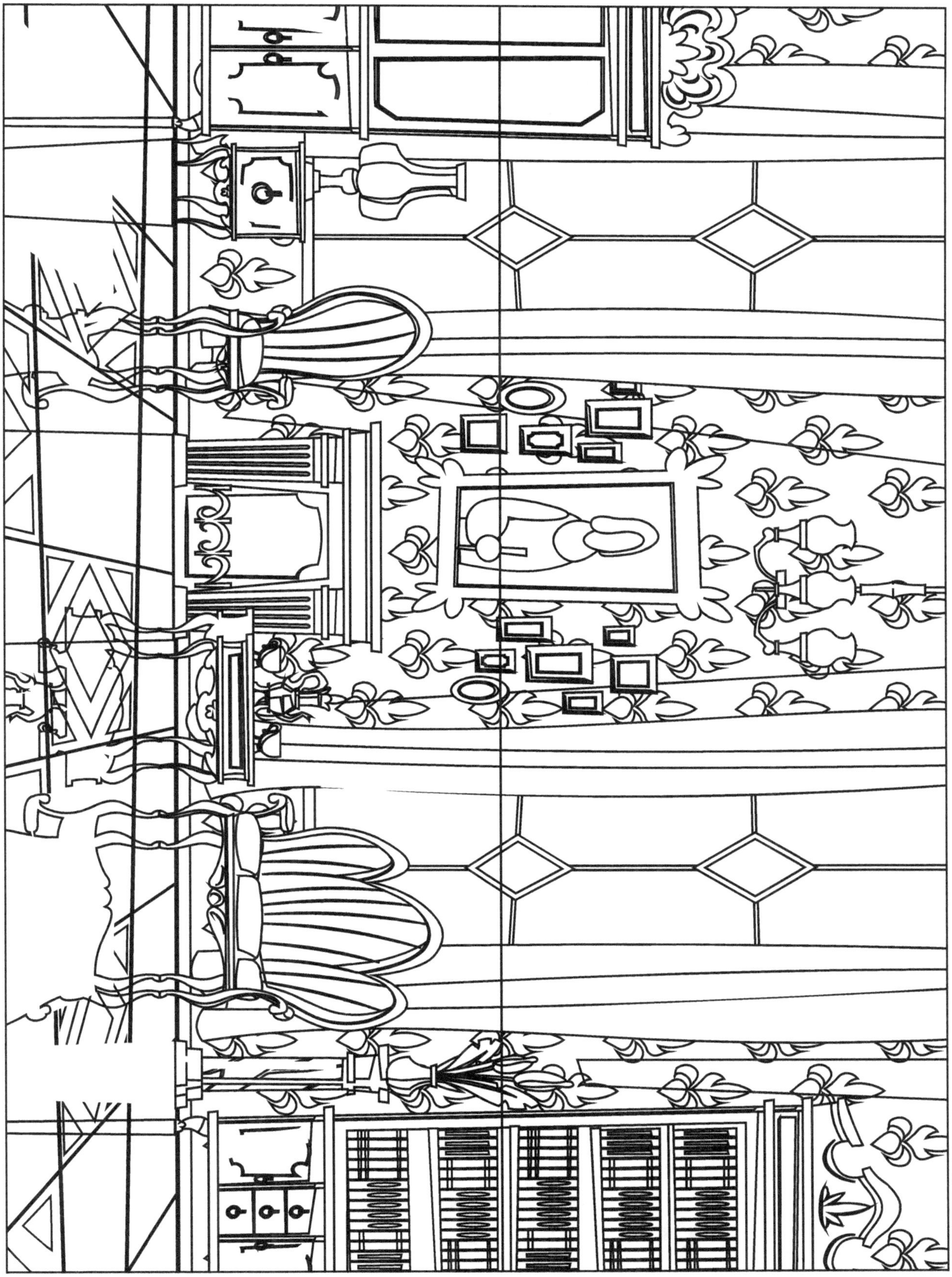

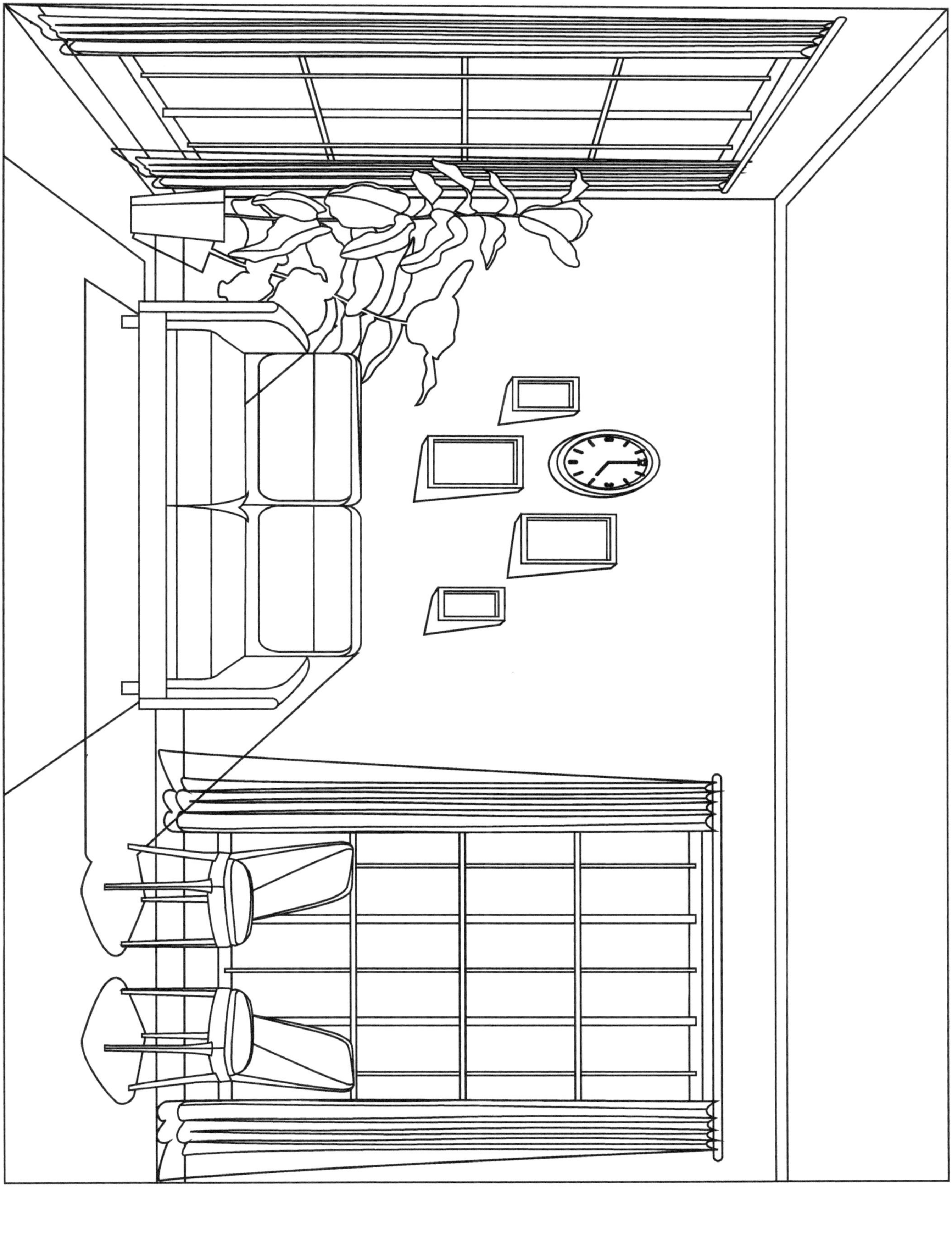

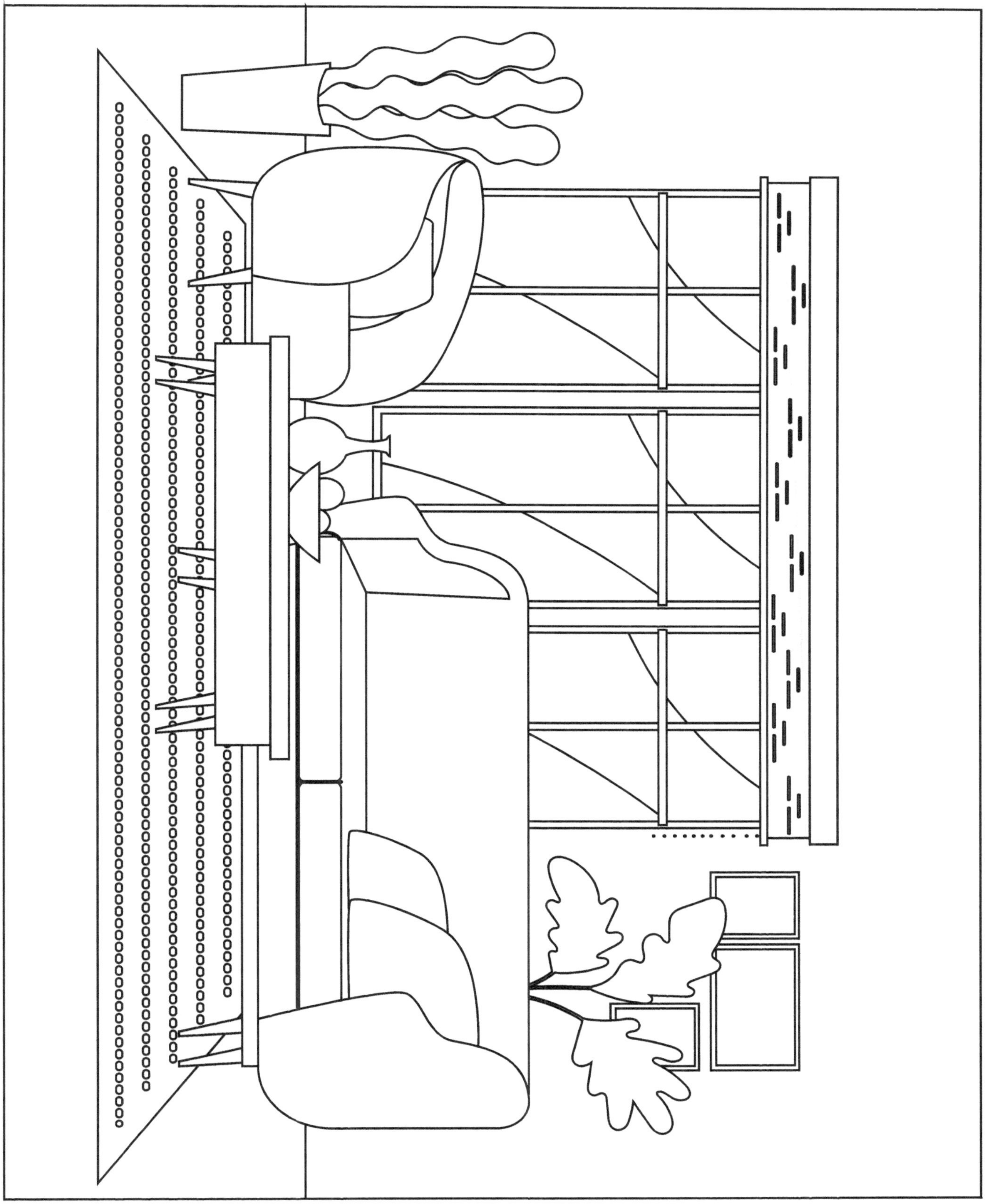

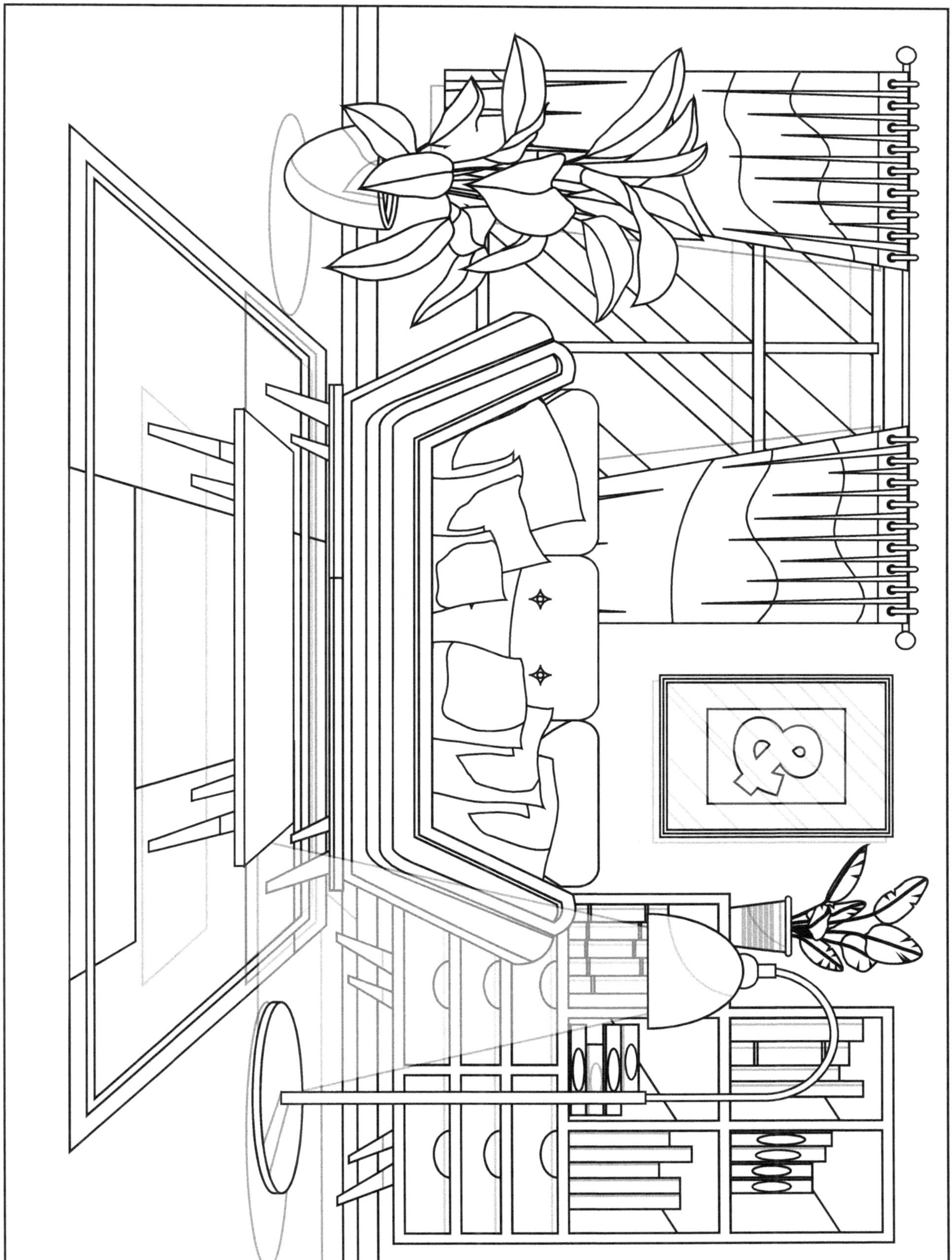

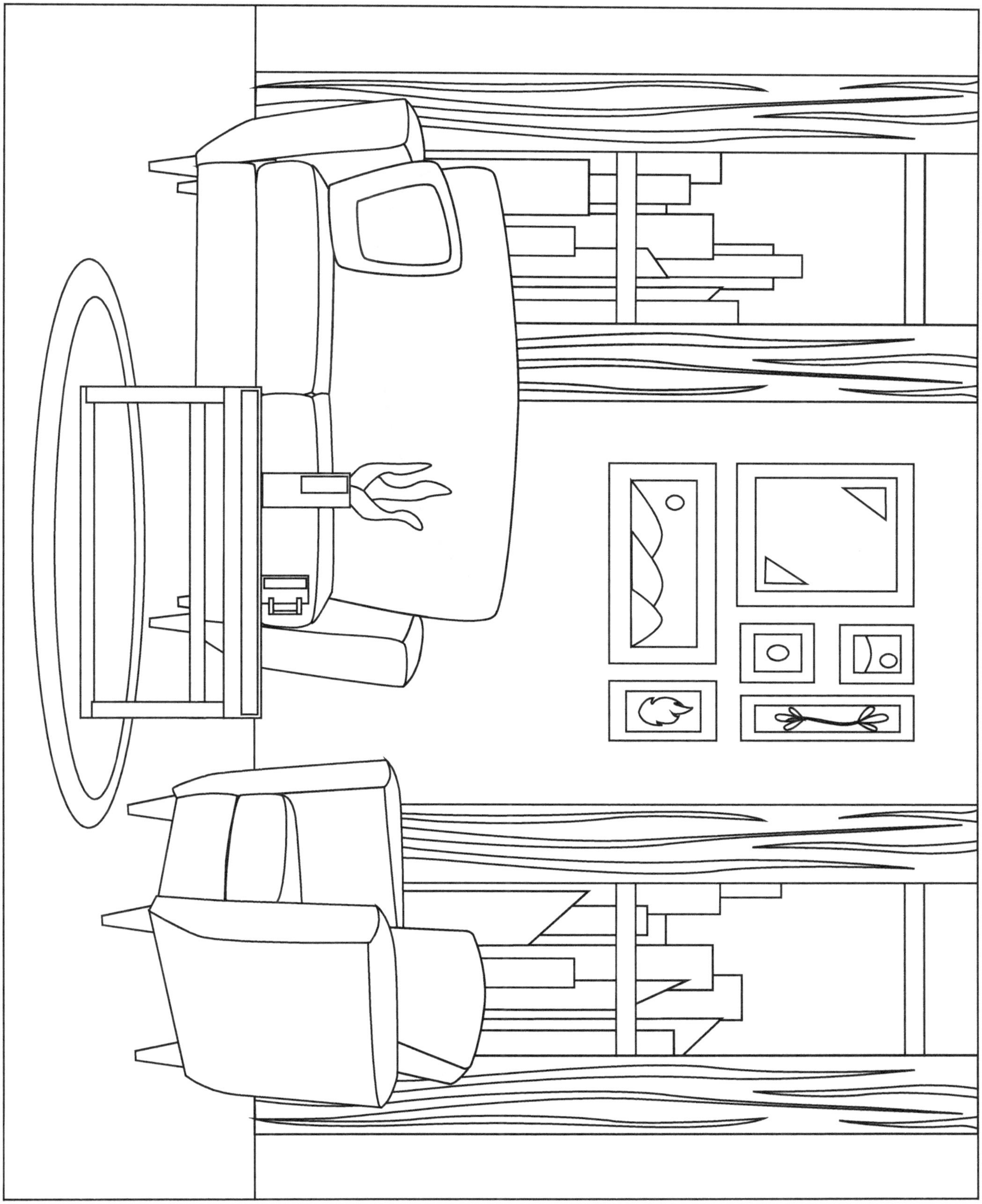

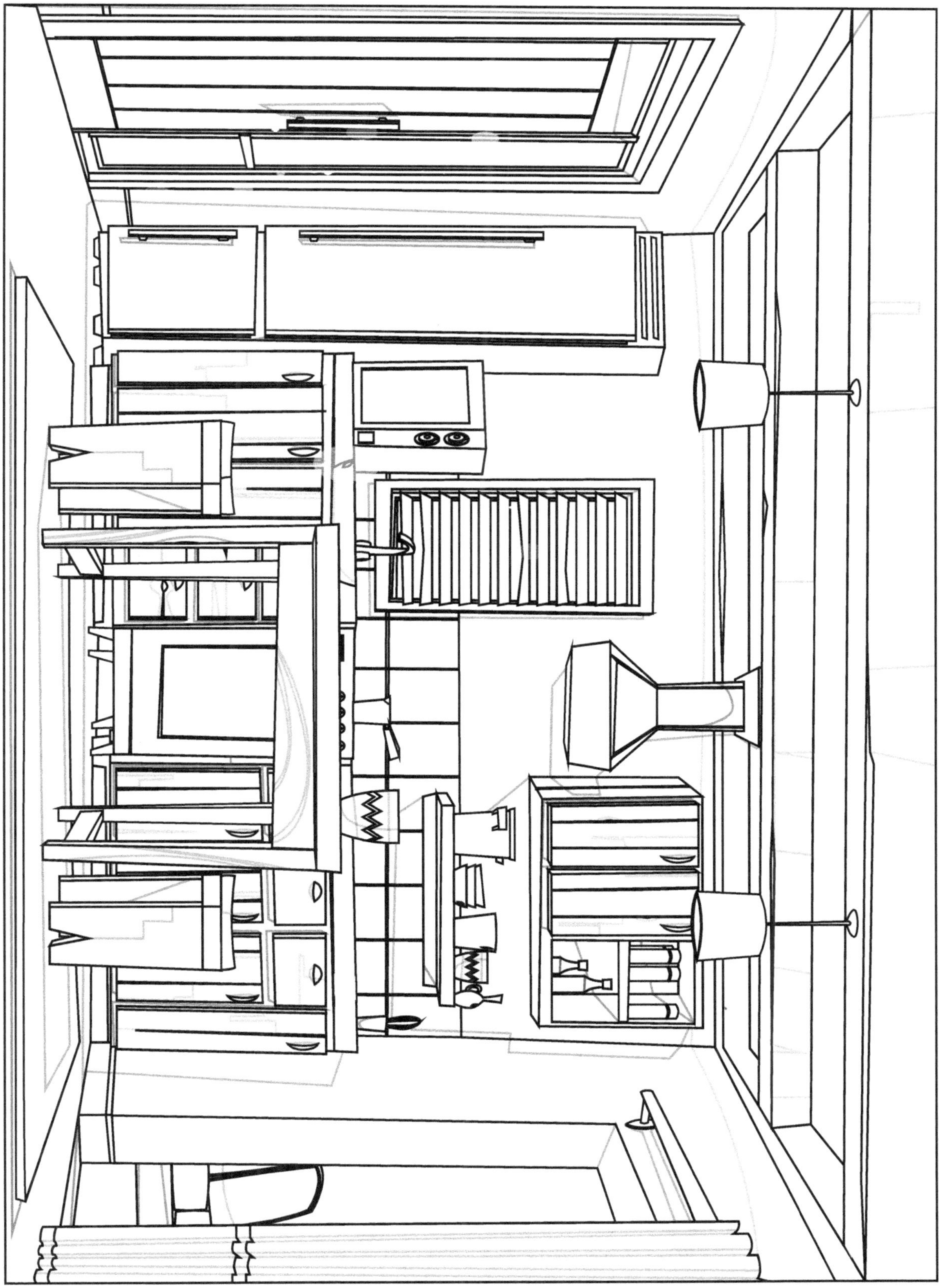

www.ingramcontent.com/pod-product-compliance
Lightning Source LLC
Chambersburg PA
CBHW080612220526
45466CB00010B/3321
979855056 5223